STECK-VAUGHN

Economics
Concepts and Applications

Larry D. Hodge

STECK-VAUGHN
ELEMENTARY · SECONDARY · ADULT · LIBRARY

A Harcourt Company

www.steck-vaughn.com

About the Author

Larry D. Hodge taught social studies in the Austin public schools before becoming a social studies editor and author. He has authored and edited social studies texts for several major publishers. He holds a B.A. in science from the University of Texas.

Acknowledgments

Cover: © Gregg Mancuso/Uniphoto (worker painting grid); © Will Stanley/TSW-Click/Chicago (oil rig); © Comstock (business meeting); © James Minor (shoppers)

p.7 © Bob Rima/Gamma-Liaison
p.8 © Michael Newman/PhotoEdit
p.10 © Lionel Delevingne/Stock, Boston
p.11 © Tom McHugh/Photo Researchers
p.12 © Chip Hires/Gamma-Liaison
p.13 © Tony Freeman/PhotoEdit
p.14 © Gale Zucker/Stock, Boston
p.17 © David Harvey/Woodfin Camp & Associates
p.18 © David Harvey/Woodfin Camp & Associates
p.19 © Ellis Herwig/Stock, Boston
p.20 © Lindsay Hebberd/Woodfin Camp & Associates
p.21 © Wendy Stone/Gamma-Liaison
p.22 © Peter Turnley/Black Star
p.26 © Antoinette Jongen/Black Star
p.27 © Antoinette Jongen/Black Star
p.29 © H. Armstrong Roberts
p.30 © Richard Hutchings/PhotoEdit
p.31 The Bettmann Archive
p.32 © Barbara Alper/Stock, Boston
p.33 © FB Grunzweig/Photo Researchers
p.34 © Spencer Grant/Stock, Boston
p.37 © Michael Dwyer/Stock, Boston
p.38 © Peter Vandermark/Stock, Boston
p.39 © Phil McCarten/PhotoEdit
p.41 © Bryce Flynn/Stock, Boston
p.42 © Michael Hayman/Stock, Boston
p.47 © Michel Philippot/Sygma
p.48 (both) The Bettmann Archive
p.49 © S. Ferry/Gamma-Liaison
p.50 © Tony Freeman/PhotoEdit
p.51 © Catherine Leroy/Sipa Press
p.54 Reuters/Bettmann Newsphotos
p.55 © Patrick Piel/Gamma-Liaison
p.57 Culver Pictures
p.58 © Michael Weisbrot/Stock, Boston
p.59 © Mike Mazzaschi/Stock, Boston
p.60 © John Coletti/Stock, Boston
p.61 © Photo Researchers
p.62 © Mike Mazzaschi/Stock, Boston
p.63 © Cynthia Ellis

p.66 © Peter Silva/Picture Group
p.67 © Fredrik Bodin/Stock, Boston
p.69 Phyllis Liedeker
p.70 © David Grossman/Photo Researchers
p.71 © Peter Menzel/Stock, Boston
p.72 © Hazel Hankin/Stock, Boston
p.76 © Mark Phillips/Photo Researchers
p.77 © Judy Canty/Stock, Boston
p.78 © Spencer Grant/Photo Researchers
p.80 © Cynthia Ellis
p.81 © Michael Dwyer/Stock, Boston
p.82 Culver Pictures
p.83 © Tom Cheek/Stock, Boston
p.86 Courtesy Ninfa's
p.87 Courtesy Ninfa's
p.89 Department of the Treasury, Bureau of Engraving
p.90 Stan Kearl
p.91 © Tony Freeman/Photo Edit
p.92 © Rhoda Sidney/PhotoEdit
p.93 © Laimute Druskis/Photo Researchers
p.94 The Library of Congress
p.95 © Lester C. King, Collection of Alabama
p.96 © Tony Freeman/PhotoEdit
p.99 © Fredrik Bodin/Stock, Boston
p.100 © Michael Hayman/Stock, Boston
p.101 © H. Armstrong Roberts
p.102 © H. Armstrong Roberts
p.103 © Owen Franken/Stock, Boston
p.104 © Judy Gelles/Stock, Boston
p.108 The Bettmann Archive
p.109 © John Neubauer/PhotoEdit
p.110 © FB Grunzweig/Photo Researchers
p.111 © Mike Mazzaschi/Stock, Boston
p.112 © Tony Sovino/Sipa Press
p.113 © Barbara Alper/Stock, Boston
p.116 (all) Courtesy American Numisematic Society
p.117 The Bettmann Archive
p.119 © Alan Oddie/PhotoEdit
p.120 © ME Warren/Photo Researchers
p.121 Culver Pictures
p.122 © John Neubauer/PhotoEdit
p.124 © Spencer Grant/Stock, Boston
p.125 Reuters/Bettmann Newsphotos
p.126 © Peter Menzel/Stock, Boston
p.129 © Cynthia Dopkin/Photo Researchers
p.130 © Tony Freeman/PhotoEdit

p.131 © Arthur Grace/Stock, Boston
p.132 © Gary Irving/TSW-Click/Chicago
p.133 © Susan Van Etten/PhotoEdit
p.134 © Jan Lukas/Photo Researchers
p.138 Culver Pictures
p.139 Culver Pictures
p.141 © Jeff Lowenthal/Woodfin Camp & Associates
p.142 © Rafael Macia/Photo Researchers
p.144 The National Archives
p.145 © Tony Freeman/PhotoEdit
p.146 © Stephen Johnson/TSW-Click/Chicago
p.147 © Mark Richards/PhotoEdit
p.150 © Christopher Johnson/Stock, Boston
p.151 © Frank Fisher/Gamma-Liaison
p.152 © Cary Wolinsky/Stock, Boston
p.153 © Fred Leavitt/TSW-Click/Chicago
p.154 © Mark Richards/PhotoEdit
p.155 © Eda Rogers/PhotoEdit
p.159 © Robert Brenner/PhotoEdit
p.160 © Tony Freeman/PhotoEdit
p.161 © H. Armstrong Roberts
p.162 Courtesy John Deere Company
p.163 AP/Wide World
p.166 © J. Mathieson/Sygma
p.167 Culver Pictures
p.169 © David Young-Wolff/PhotoEdit
p.170 © Spencer Grant/Stock, Boston
p.171 © Rafael Macia/Photo Researchers
p.172 © Paul Conklin/PhotoEdit
p.173 © Christopher Morrow/Stock, Boston
p.174 © Peter Menzel/Stock, Boston
p.175 © H. Armstrong Roberts
p.179 © Bob Daemmerich
p.180 © H. Armstrong Roberts
p.181 © H. Armstrong Roberts
p.182 © Eugene Mopsik/H. Armstrong Roberts
p.183 © Bob Daemmerich
p.184 © Ellis Herwig/Stock, Boston
p.185 © H. Armstrong Roberts
p.188 © Charles Kennard/Stock, Boston
p.189 © Calvin Larsen/Photo Researchers
Pages 138-139 from The Jungle by Upton Sinclair, published by Penguin Books USA Inc.

Pages 6, 28, 56, 88, 118, 140, 168 Illustrations by Gary McElhaney

Consultants:

Arne Kildegaard: Dr. Kildegaard is an assistant professor in economics at Tulane University of Louisiana.

Ann Grabhorn-Friday, M.Ed.: Ms. Grabhorn-Friday has taught economics at the high-school level in Austin, TX.

Staff Credits:

Executive Editor: Diane Sharpe
Design Manager: Cynthia Ellis
Photo Editor: Margie Foster
Production: Go Media, Inc.

Table of Contents

To the Reader

Who decides what is for sale at the department store? You do! Every time you buy something, you are telling the seller that what you buy is worth selling. Without you, the buyer, businesses would go out of business. So they do whatever they can to satisfy you.

The economy of the United States depends on people like you and the people who provide those things that are for sale. The economy does well when businesses provide many things for sale, and when buyers buy them. Sometimes the economy does not do so well. What makes it change?

In *Economics: Concepts and Applications* you will read about all parts of the economy. You will learn what causes the economy to do well one year and not so well the next.

You will read about the kind of economy we have in the United States. And you will read about other economies in other nations.

You will read about banks and how they do business. You will learn about money and its role in the economy.

Finally you will learn about how the economy in the United States depends on economies in other nations. You will read about trade and how nations decide what to trade.

Every time you make a purchase, you affect the economy. As you read, think about other ways you are a part of the economy. Think about all the ways the economy affects your life.

UNIT
I

INTRODUCTION to ECONOMICS

At some point in the distant past, people might have had all the food, clothing, and other things they wanted. But it is unlikely. During most of human history, people have wanted more than they have had. They have not been able to get all they wanted because there is not enough of everything to go around. People have had to make choices about what they had to have and what they could do without. The story of the human race is largely the story of how people have used work, wits, and war to get the things they want.

In 1990, the leader of Iraq invaded the tiny nation of Kuwait. That tiny nation has a huge supply of oil. People all over the world depend on oil from Kuwait and other nations to drive, to heat and cool their homes, and to run machines in factories. So people were angry when Kuwait was invaded. They were afraid the cost of oil would become very high. Many nations joined together to fight Iraq and force its army to leave Kuwait. Those nations were successful. One reason those nations went to war was economics.

Economics — how people satisfy their needs and wants — has been a powerful force in history. As people began to want more, they had to face the fact that there was not always enough to go around. People have struggled with others over land, oil, gold, fishing rights, and more. Every country tries to provide for its people. How countries do that is the story of economics.

Have You Ever Wondered...

- Why can't you always have everything you want?
- Why must you sometimes choose between two things rather than have them both?
- Who decides what products are offered in stores?
- Who decides whether you will be able to buy certain things?

All of those questions will be answered in this unit. You will read about the difference between things we want and things we need. You will learn that because the earth's resources are limited we cannot have everything we want. You will learn about how people decide what should be produced, how it should be produced, and who should get it. As you read this unit, think about yourself and how you fit into our economic system.

The BASICS of ECONOMICS

CHAPTER 1

Consider as you read

- Why can't we have everything we want?
- How are all goods and services made?

Think of all the things you have. You have clothes, food, and a home. Perhaps you have a bicycle, a stereo, or a pet. You probably have many other things, too.

Ask yourself which of these things you could do without. Can you do without food? You could for a while, but not for long. Food is something you must have in order to live. Food is something we call a **need**.

Even though you may have a great many things, you probably do not have everything you would like to have. Would you like to have all the tapes of your favorite musical group? You may feel that you cannot live without the tapes, but in truth, you can. They would be nice to have, but you can live without them. For you, the tapes are something we call a **want**.

need
something we can't live without

want
something we would like to have

Are these students buying something they want or something they need?

8

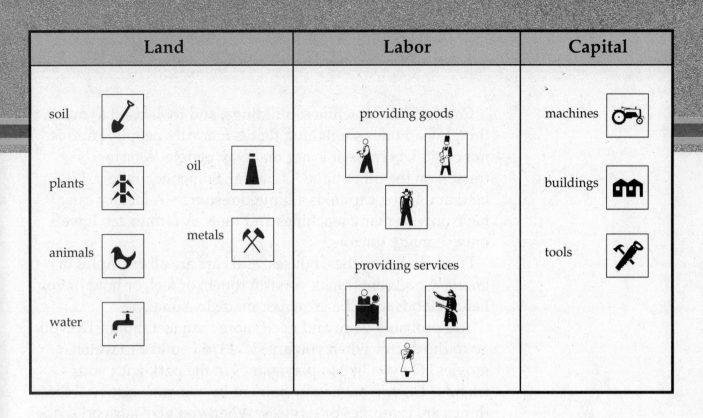

Land	Labor	Capital
soil	providing goods	machines
plants		buildings
oil		
animals		tools
metals		
water	providing services	

Wants and Needs Are Produced from Limited Resources

We live in a world with **limited resources**. We use resources to make or get the things we need and want. Resources can be divided into three groups: **land**, **labor**, and **capital**. Everything we need or want is produced using these three things. Land, labor, and capital are called the **factors of production**.

Land resources include more than just land itself. Soil, of course, is an important resource. It lets us grow food. Also part of the land are plants, animals, water, oil, and metals. All these things can be taken from the land. But the amount of land, water, oil, and so on is limited. If we use steel to make new cars, we can't use that same steel to build new schools or bridges. We have to make a choice. Do we want new cars or new bridges?

Labor is the work people do with their hands and their minds. Carpenters build houses with their hands. Singers make music with their minds and voices. The carpenter provides a **good**. The singer provides a **service**. Both are part of the resource we call labor. Labor is also a limited resource. Not everyone is a good carpenter or singer. You probably wouldn't want a house built by your favorite singer, and you probably wouldn't want to listen to your carpenter sing. Since not everyone can do everything well, labor is a limited resource.

limited
only a certain amount

resources
things used to provide what we need or want

land
things in nature

labor
work

capital
goods used to make other goods

factors of production
three kinds of resources needed for making things

good
something that is made by people

service
action people do for others

Capital is the machines, buildings, and tools used to make things. Capital is something that is made by people. Land is not capital, because it is not made by people. A farmer's tractor, on the other hand, is capital. Someone made it. Like land and labor, capital is a limited resource. A factory can have only so many machines and tools. A farmer can have only so many tractors.

Food, water, clothes, houses, and cars are all examples of goods. Goods are things you can touch, or feel, or hold in your hand. Goods must be grown or made by someone.

You probably want and need more than just things. Do you go to the doctor when you are sick? Do you like to watch movies? Do you like to play games in the park with your friends? Do you have your hair cut by someone else? All these things are examples of services. When you give a friend a ride, you are performing a service. When you buy a ticket to see a movie, you are buying a service. You are not paying for the movie. You are paying for the service of someone showing you the movie.

Land, labor, and capital all work together to produce the goods and services we need. A good such as a house is made of wood and stone from the land. Workers put these materials together with their labor. The workers use capital such as hammers, saws, trucks, and other equipment in their work.

This carpenter is providing a service.

Land, labor, and capital go into producing a good such as a car.

In the case of services, imagine a musical group giving a concert. The place where the concert is held is land. The singing and playing of the band members is labor. The building where the concert is held is capital.

Of course, houses don't just get built by themselves. The wood and stone for a house don't just appear on the building site. Concerts don't just happen. Things happen because people make them happen. Goods and services are provided because people work to meet the needs and wants of themselves and other people.

The Problem of Scarcity

People all over the world have many of the same needs and wants. Most people would like to have a better house, more food, or nicer clothes. However, most people do not have everything they would like to have. Why is this? Why can't you have everything you want?

The answer is simply that people have so many needs and wants that there often isn't enough to go around. Limited resources mean that we can't produce everything that everybody wants. There isn't enough flour and cheese, for example, for everybody in the world to have all the pizza they want. There isn't enough steel in the world for every person to have all the cars he or she wants. There is a **scarcity** of many things. When there is a scarcity of something, there is not enough for everyone.

scarcity
lack

11

Scarcity of resources is a problem we all face. Often it means we cannot have everything we want. Since resources are scarce, the goods made from them are also scarce. If floods wipe out a potato crop, there may be a scarcity of potato chips. Sometimes scarcity means that we cannot have everything we need. If you are lost in a desert, you may have a scarcity of water.

Making Choices

Everything we want or need is either a good or a service. Scarcity means that we cannot have all the goods and services we would like to have. Therefore, we must make choices. Perhaps you have been saving to buy new shoes to wear to a special party. You finally have enough money to buy the shoes. On your way to the store, you notice that a movie you have been wanting to see for months is showing. If you go to see the movie, you will not have enough money to pay for the shoes. You must choose. Will you see the movie or buy the shoes?

We all face such choices each day. If we spend our lunch money on a new book, we will go hungry. On the other hand, if we don't buy the book, we will miss the enjoyment of reading it.

If there is a scarcity of a resource, people may have to wait to get it. Here people are waiting for gas.

The opportunity cost for this man of buying tomatoes could be corn or peas.

The value of things you give up when you make choices is called **opportunity cost**. If you go to a movie instead of buying shoes, the opportunity cost is the shoes you gave up. If you buy lunch instead of a book, the opportunity cost is the missed enjoyment of reading.

Opportunity costs can sometimes be very great. Suppose that your town needs a new school, but it also needs a new bridge to replace an old one that is dangerous. There is only enough money for either a school or a bridge, but not both. If the new school is built, the old bridge may fall and hurt someone. The opportunity cost is the problem caused by failure of the bridge. If the new school is not built, students may not learn as much as they might have. The lost learning is the opportunity cost of the new bridge.

opportunity cost
something that is given up in order to have something else

Three Basic Economic Activities

An economic activity is anything people do to meet wants and needs. The things people do to provide goods and services can be divided into three groups. We call these groups the basic economic activities. The three groups are:
1. taking materials from the earth,
2. making things, and
3. providing services.

People who take things from the earth include farmers, miners, and fishers. Farmers grow crops using soil and water.

manufacturing
making

Miners dig or drill into the earth for metals, oil, stone, and other resources. Fishers gather food from the earth's rivers, lakes, and oceans. You will find many goods from the earth in grocery stores.

Making things is often called **manufacturing**. We call things that are made manufactured goods. Manufactured goods include things like steel, cars, television sets, clothes, chairs, toys, and thousands of other things. Manufactured goods are things that cannot be grown or taken from the earth. A department store is filled with manufactured goods.

Services can take many forms. Doctors, lawyers, and teachers provide services. So do restaurants, dry cleaners, and auto repair shops. When you get a haircut or play a video game, you are buying a service.

By now you are probably wondering about something. If scarcity forces us all to make choices, who decides what goods and services get produced? How do farmers know what crops to grow? How do factories know what manufactured goods to make? How do people decide what services to offer? These and other questions will be answered later in this book.

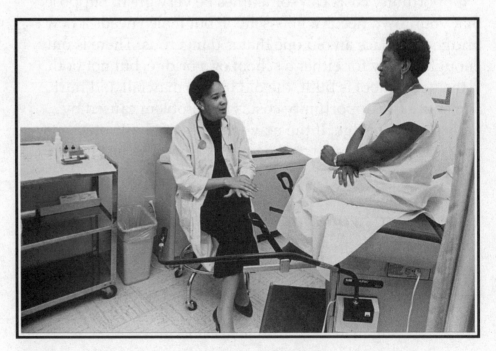

Providing a service is one of the three basic economic activities.

Comprehension – *Write the Answer*

Write one or more sentences to answer each question.

1. What are three things you have that could be called needs? _____

_____

2. What are three things you have that could be called wants? _____

_____

3. What are the factors of production? _____

_____

_____

4. What is the difference between goods and services? _____

_____

_____

5. What are the three basic economic activities? _____

_____

_____

Vocabulary – *Exclusions*

One word or phrase in each group does not belong. Find that word and cross it out.
Then write a sentence that tells how the other words are alike.

1. clothing
   food
   water
   music

   _____

   _____

   _____

2. soil
   machines
   oil
   plants

   _____

   _____

3. taking materials from the earth _____
   manufacturing
   making choices   _____
   providing services
                                    _____

4. farmers   _____
   doctors
   miners   _____
   fishers
                                    _____

Critical Thinking– *Fact and Opinion*

A **fact** is a true statement. An **opinion** is a statement that tells what a person thinks.

> **Fact:** We live in a world with limited resources.
> **Opinion:** We should be allowed to have as much as we want of anything.

Read each sentence below. If the sentence is a fact, write **F** on the blank. If the sentence is an opinion, write **O** on the blank. If the sentence gives both a fact and an opinion, write **FO** on the blank, and circle the part of the sentence that is an opinion.

_____ 1. We cannot do without some things.

_____ 2. Limited resources should be shared equally among all people.

_____ 3. Land, labor, and capital are all types of resources, but capital is the most useful resource.

_____ 4. Land, labor, and capital all go into each good or service we need.

_____ 5. If we all worked together, we could do away with scarcity.

_____ 6. Grocery stores should sell only things taken from the earth.

_____ 7. Doctors offer the most important services.

_____ 8. Knowing opportunity costs can help us make choices.

_____ 9. Land is one factor of production.

_____ 10. Bus drivers provide a service that is more important in big cities than in small cities.

16

FOUR
ECONOMIC SYSTEMS

CHAPTER 2

Consider as you read

- How does economics work?
- How do you describe different economic systems?

Scarcity is the basic economic problem you face. You will never be able to buy everything you want. Even very rich people may be unable to have everything they want. For example, all people can get sick. And no amount of money can buy a person good health.

It may surprise you to know that even nations have to deal with scarcity. In recent years India, China, and other countries have often not had enough food. The United States has not been able to produce all the oil it needs. In some countries there are not enough doctors or schools.

Nations, like people, have to make choices. Sometimes the choices are very hard to make. For example, a country's

In order to grow more crops, some people have to clear away the forest.

people may need more food. One way to grow more food is to burn forests and plant crops on the land. But smoke from burning forests makes the air dirty. Once the trees are cut, rain may wash away the dirt, making the land useless in a few years. Which is more important — clean air and good soil or food?

Think about this. A nation feels it must be strong to protect itself from warlike neighbors. So the nation's leaders use most of the country's land, labor, and capital to build guns, tanks, ships, and planes. Because few tractors are made, farmers cannot grow enough food. Factories cannot get material to make enough clothes. People have to live in poor houses, because few new ones are built. Would you be surprised to learn that people in that nation might be very unhappy with their leaders?

These things have happened in recent years. Brazil has faced problems because of the burning of its forests. People in many countries in Eastern Europe and other parts of the world have been very unhappy because they have had to live in small houses without enough food.

Three Basic Questions of Economics

Every nation must answer three questions about goods and services. We call these questions the three basic questions of

Here, people are mining for the resource copper.

Labor and capital, in the form of farm equipment, are needed to turn the land into farmland.

economics. The questions are:

1. What goods and services should be produced?
2. How should these goods and services be produced?
3. Who will get the goods and services?

Answering these three questions is not easy. In fact, every country's leaders spend a great deal of time every day trying to answer these questions in the way they think is best for their country.

Suppose a country needs more oil. You might think that the country would answer the question "What goods and services should be produced?" by saying "More oil." However, what if the country does not have any oil? The country cannot produce more oil just because the oil is needed.

How a country answers the first question also depends on what it hopes to do as a country. For example, one country may want to provide more food for its people. This country may choose to produce more tractors and farm equipment. Another country may also want to provide more food. But it may not have enough land to grow food. This country may choose to produce tanks and planes and take land from another country. Or it may choose to build factories, make goods, sell them to other countries, and use the money to buy the food it needs.

The question "How should these goods and services be produced?" is also hard to answer. The answer depends on how a nation chooses to use its land, labor, and capital. Some countries may produce most of their goods using machines. In other countries, most goods may be made by hand.

Once goods and services have been produced, they must be divided up among the people of the country. The third question is "Who will get the goods and services?" Will everyone be given an equal share? Will some people get more than others?

Kinds of Economic Systems

How a country answers the three basic economic questions tells a great deal about that country. Each country has an **economic system**. An economic system is the rules a country follows in answering the three basic questions. There are four kinds of economic systems.

A **traditional economy** makes decisions based on what has been done in the past. People produce the goods and services they have always produced. People may herd cattle because their family has always herded cattle. One village may produce clay pots because people who live there have always made them. The question "How should goods and services be

economic system
the way a country answers the basic questions

traditional economy
economic system in which decisions are made based on what has always been done

Some people choose to make goods by hand. These women in India are weaving cloth.

20

This farm in Africa is part of a traditional economy.

produced?" is answered in the same way. If a girl's mother made rugs with a particular pattern, the girl will make the same kind of rugs using the same methods. People in this kind of economy usually share equally in the goods and services provided. Thus the answer to the third question is, "Everyone gets the same amount."

In a **command economy**, government leaders decide the answers to the basic economic questions. The government controls the land, labor, and capital, the three factors of production. The government decides what and how much of each item will be made. It decides where people will work, whether they will use machines or do work by hand, and how much they will be paid. Finally, the government decides who will be able to buy the goods and services that are produced.

A **market economy** is the opposite of a command economy. In a market economy, each person answers the three basic questions. People may buy and sell whatever they like. People decide for themselves whether they will make things by hand or by machine.

The most important part of a market economy is the **market**. A market is the means by which goods and services are bought and sold freely. For example, a person who has an item for sale is free to sell it to anyone who will buy it. In a market system, therefore, people usually produce goods that other

command economy
economic system in which the decisions are made by the government

market economy
economic system in which decisions are made by each person

market
how goods and services are bought and sold

people will want to buy. This answers the question of what to produce. How goods will be produced is up to the person making them. One person may make tables by hand while another may make them using machines. Who gets the goods depends on who is willing and able to buy them. The person who wants a cheap table may buy one made by machine. The person who wants a table that is not like any other may buy one made by hand.

Most nations in the world today have a **mixed economy**. A mixed economy is one which is part command and part market economy. Most governments have some say over how the three basic economic questions are answered. However, many decisions are left up to the people. The United States has a mixed economy. You will read more about mixed economies in the next unit.

These apple growers are part of a command economy.

Vocabulary — *Match Up*

Choose a word or phrase from the box to complete each sentence. Write that word or phrase on the blank.

market economy	three basic questions	traditional economy
economic system	command economy	mixed economy

1. Government leaders spend a great deal of time trying to answer

   the _____ of economics.

2. The rules a country follows in answering questions about what to produce, how

   to produce it, and who gets it make up that country's _____ .

3. Decisions in a _____ are based on what has been done in
   the past.

4. Government leaders decide the answers to the three basic questions

   in a _____ .

5. People may make, buy, and sell whatever they like in

   a _____ .

6. Most nations today have a _____ .

Comprehension — *Write a Paragraph*

Use six or more words or phrases in the box to write a paragraph that explains the differences between a command and a market economy.

government	market	control
factors of production	command	economy
goods	services	three basic questions

_____

_____

_____

_____

_____

_____

Critical Thinking – *Drawing Conclusions*

To draw a **conclusion**, you need to see how information fits together and gives a paragraph meaning. To draw a correct conclusion, you must be sure it is supported by the paragraph.

Read the paragraph below and the sentences that follow it. Put a check in front of the conclusions that can be drawn from the paragraph.

> In a command economy, the government owns the land and the factories. It tells workers where they must work. It tells people how much of each item to make. Government decides how much people will be paid. It even controls who can buy goods and services.

_____ 1. People do not have much economic freedom in a command economy.

_____ 2. A person cannot change jobs unless the government says so.

_____ 3. People do not like to live in a command economy.

_____ 4. Government leaders answer the basic economic questions in a command economy.

_____ 5. Government controls mean that everyone has an equal chance to buy goods and services.

Reading a Bar Graph

The bar graph below shows the average length of people's lives in six countries. Study the graph. Then answer the questions.

How Long People Live in Traditional and Modern Economies

India — 57
United States — 75
Peru — 62
Japan — 78
Libya — 58
Sweden — 76

1. What countries are shown on the graph? _____

_____

2. In which country shown do people live the least number of years? _____

_____

3. In which country shown do people live the most number of years? _____

_____

4. How much longer can someone in Japan expect to live than someone in Peru?

_____

5. What is the difference between the shortest and longest length of life shown?

_____

6. In most traditional economies, there are few doctors, so many people share one doctor. People may have to wait a long time to see their doctor. They may not get good medical care. Based on the graph, which countries shown do you think have traditional economies? Why? _____

_____

_____

Life in a Traditional Economy

People who live in a traditional economy do not have to answer questions like "What work will I do when I grow up? Should I change jobs? Can I buy that item? Will I try to be rich?" Life in a traditional economy is simple. People do not have a lot of worries. However, peace of mind does have an opportunity cost. Life in a traditional economy can be hard. There may be few choices to make, but there are also few freedoms. Let's visit people living in a traditional economy and see how they live for just one day.

The sun is hot, and the rocks are heavy. Mahmud is working with his father. They have to clear rocks from the field before plowing it. They have only their hands and backs to lift the rocks. It will take many days to clear the field. It will take many days more to plow the earth. The wooden plow with a metal tip will be pulled by two oxen.

Mahmud never wonders why they work in this way. People in his village have always farmed in this way. His father's father had done the same. Crops are small. Often people are hungry. Sometimes children or old people die from hunger. No one asks why. It has always been so.

Mahmud watches his father carefully as they work. He must learn how to do the work. Mahmud's sister works with their mother. She learns to cook the meals they have always eaten. Much of each day is spent weaving cloth. The colors and patterns in the cloth are ones people in the village have always used.

Once a week the family goes to a larger village. People from other small villages come, too. Each family brings things to trade. A piece of cloth might be traded for some chickens. A bag of rice might be traded for a piece of

People in traditional economies do things in the same way that their families have always done them.

metal. Mahmud's father will use the metal to make a new knife. He will use the knife to cut grass to feed their oxen. It will take a long time to make the knife. The blade will be ground into shape by rubbing the metal over a stone. Someday Mahmud will make a knife in the same way. He does not wonder if there is a better, quicker way to make a knife.

In the evening the family sits around a small fire for a time before going to bed. There is no electricity in the village. Mahmud's father tells stories he heard from his father. The stories are about people who had lived long ago. Sometimes they sing songs. Mahmud's mother learned the songs from her mother. Mahmud does not understand some of the songs, but singing them makes him feel good. He feels part of the family. In his world the family is the most important thing. The family takes care of children. It takes care of old people.

Mahmud lives the same way his parents and grandparents did. His children will probably live the same way.

❖

Write About It

On a separate piece of paper, write a paragraph that tells how your life in a mixed economy is different from life in a traditional economy.

Without modern machines, a job such as harvesting grain takes many long hours.

UNIT

CAPITALISM, COMMUNISM, and SOCIALISM

While many countries still have traditional economic systems, command and free enterprise sytems play leading roles in the world today. Free enterprise is the economic system in the United States. Americans have had free enterprise since before the United States even became a nation. Communism began in Russia in 1917. The idea of communism came from one man — Karl Marx.

After communists seized power in Russia in 1917, communists and capitalists became locked in a struggle. Each side tried to prove that its system worked best. How much control should government have over people's lives? Communists believe government should have a great deal of control. Capitalists argue that people should be allowed to decide most things for themselves. By 1992 the communists no longer controlled Russia.

In a communist system, the government answers the three questions. People carry out the decisions made by the government. In a free enterprise system, the people, as producers or consumers, answer the three questions.

As the leading capitalist country in the world, the United States has played a big part in the struggle between capitalism and communism. In recent years capitalism is found in more and more nations, but the arguments over which economic system is best will probably continue.

Have You Ever Wondered...

- What are the differences between capitalism, socialism, and communism?

- Where does money go after you have spent it?

- Who decides what goods on store shelves are for sale?

- Why do stores have sales on some things and charge high prices for others?

These questions and many others will be answered in this unit. You will read about Adam Smith and Karl Marx, men who had very different ideas about economics. You will learn how you are the most important person in a free enterprise system. You will learn why giant businesses want to know what you think. You will learn why the choices you make every day are an important part of the free enterprise system. You will read about how people in other countries live under socialism and communism.

CAPITALISM and FREE ENTERPRISE

CHAPTER 3

Consider as you read

- What makes a market work?
- What keeps people who make goods from charging high prices for them?
- How do people who buy goods help make the market work?

Because most nations today have a mixed economy, you might think that all economies would be alike. But this is not the case. Some mixed economies have a great deal of government control. Others have very little control.

In a few countries, almost all businesses are owned by people acting for themselves. The factors of production are owned mostly by people, not the government. The government does have some control over the economy. However, this control is very limited. This kind of economy is called **capitalism**. In capitalism, the market is the important part of the economy. Capitalism is practiced in the United States.

capitalism
economic system in the United States

In capitalism, buyers are part of the market.

Adam Smith Explains Market Economies

How does a market system work? There are over two hundred million people in the United States. How do they tell businesses what to produce? Could you call an auto maker and tell it to whip up a sporty car just for you? Of course you couldn't. But in a way, every time you do or do not buy something, you are telling businesses what to make.

Adam Smith lived in Scotland over two hundred years ago. Market economies were just beginning then. He wondered how they worked. After studying market economies, he wrote a book to explain them. His book was called *The Wealth of Nations*. It is still an important book.

First Smith looked at how people make decisions. How does a person who makes things decide what to make? How does a person shopping for something decide what to buy? Smith said that each person makes decisions based on **self-interest**.

Suppose you want to buy a new coat. The store has two coats that look just alike. They seem to be made just alike. You think that one is just as good as the other. But one coat costs $10 less than the other. Which will you buy? Smith said you will buy the cheaper coat because it is in your self-interest to do so. If you buy the cheaper coat, you will save money.

Now look at the same problem from the point of view of people who make coats. Suppose you make coats. If your coats cost too much, they will not sell. If the coats do not sell, you will not make money. What will you try to do? Of course,

self-interest
what is best for each person

you will try to make coats that will sell. You will try to make better, cheaper coats than anyone else. You will try to outdo all the other coat makers so that you will sell more coats than they do. This is in your self-interest.

Adam Smith said that it is as if an invisible hand controls market economies. This invisible hand is self-interest. Smith believed that if each person does what is best for him or her, everyone will benefit. He said that there is little need for government controls on the economy. If each person acts in his or her own self-interest, the best interests of everyone will be served.

What Makes Market Economies Work

In a market system, **consumers** and **producers** together answer the basic economic questions. They decide what is produced, how it is produced, and who gets it. Four things make the market system work. These things are competition, profit, private property, and freedom of exchange.

Competition is a key feature of a market system. In a market system, producers compete with one another. Producers try to make their goods cheaper and better than anyone else. Think of all the ads you see every day on television, in newspapers, and in store windows. Most of the ads promise you better goods, lower prices, or both. Producers and stores do this because they must compete with each other for your business.

consumers
people who buy goods and services

producers
people who provide goods and services

competition
when one person tries to outdo another

Producers get buyers to buy goods by using ads like these.

People can choose to sell their private property.

Why would people go to all the trouble to build a giant factory to make things? Why would they spend a lot of money to advertise? Why would they do everything they could to get you to buy their products? The answer is **profit**. Profit is why producers work so hard to get your business.

Think of yourself. Would you work hard every day if you got nothing for your work? Most people work because they get paid for working. If you have a job, you expect a paycheck. If you don't get paid, you will quit. For producers, profit is their paycheck. If they make a profit, they will keep on making things. If they don't make a profit, they will quit.

As you can see, profit and competition work together. The desire for profit makes producers compete. If producers want to make profits, they must compete for consumers' money. They do this by making better goods, by charging less, or both. This helps consumers, who get better goods at lower prices.

Private property is also important in a market system. A person's house, car, and clothes are private property. A business can own buildings and machines. The government does not own private property.

The important thing about private property is that people can use it as they wish. They can sell it if they like. People can buy as much private property as they can afford.

profit
money remaining after costs are paid; money the producer keeps

private property
goods owned by people or by businesses

Can you see why private property is important in a market system? Think what it would be like if you could not own private property. Would you work hard at a job if you could not buy anything with the money you made? Would producers compete for your money if they could not keep their profits? Private property is the reason people work to make money. People work to get a better house, better clothes, better food, or a better car. Buying private property is how people serve their own self-interest. And as Adam Smith said, self-interest is the invisible hand that guides market economies.

freedom of exchange
the freedom to buy and sell at any price

The last part of a market system is **freedom of exchange**. Producers can set whatever price they want on their goods. Consumers are free to decide whether or not to pay the price. Producers want to sell their goods, so they set prices that consumers will pay. Competition keeps producers from charging prices that are too high.

You deal with freedom of exchange every day. You may shop around before you buy clothes or food. Just because someone offers something for sale does not mean you have to buy it. If pizza at one store is too high, you can go to another where it is cheaper.

free enterprise
system in which producers and consumers decide what is in the nation's best interest

In a market economy, we the people make most decisions about what will be produced, how it will be produced, and who will get it. We call this **free enterprise**. The United States has free enterprise. In the next chapter, you will learn more about how the American free enterprise system works.

Producers set whatever price they want on goods, but consumers choose whether or not to pay that price.

Comprehension — *Write the Questions*

Below are the answers for some questions from this chapter. Read each answer. Then write your own question above each answer. Use the question words to help you.

1. What _____ ?
   This kind of economy is controlled mainly by the market.

2. Why _____ ?
   He wanted to explain how market economies work.

3. What _____ ?
   People base decisions on this thing.

4. Who _____ ?
   Producers and consumers decide what is produced, how it is produced, and who gets it.

5. Why _____ ?
   People hope to make a profit.

6. Why _____ ?
   People hope to own private property.

7. What _____ ?
   These goods are owned by people or businesses.

8. What _____ ?
   Producers can charge any price, and consumers can pay any price.

Vocabulary — *Find the Meaning*

Write the word or phrase that best completes each sentence on the blank.

1. In capitalism the _____ is the main control of the economy.
   government   market   people

2. According to Adam Smith, people make decisions based on _____.
   the market   self-interest   price

3. Adam Smith wrote about the _____ hand.

    visible   undivided   invisible

4. Consumers are the people who _____ things.

    sell   make   buy

5. Producers are the people who _____ things.

    move   make   buy

6. Producers _____ each other by lowering prices and using ads.

    compete with   argue with   outsmart

7. Profit is _____ left over after all costs are paid.

    money   goods   prices

8. Because we can buy private property, we are willing to _____ .

    compete for jobs   shop for better prices   work to make money

9. Freedom of exchange lets us _____ for better goods and prices.

    work hard   shop around   make higher profits

Critical Thinking – *Drawing Conclusions*

Read the paragraph below and the sentences that follow it. Put a check in front of the conclusions that can be drawn from the paragraph.

> In a market system, everyone competes with everyone else. Each person tries to serve his or her self-interest. Producers try to make the highest profits. Consumers try to buy at the lowest prices. People are free to use their money to buy private property.

_____ 1. Competition is important in a market system.

_____ 2. It is in a producer's self-interest to make profits.

_____ 3. Consumers would rather pay high prices than low prices.

_____ 4. A market system would not work without freedom of exchange.

_____ 5. Market systems have some government controls.

The FREE ENTERPRISE SYSTEM

CHAPTER 4

Consider as you read

- How do consumers affect what producers make?
- How do producers and consumers work together in a market?
- What is the relationship between the money you spend and the money you earn?

If you are like most people, you want many things. Often when you want something, you go to a store and buy it. Sometimes many people want the same things you want. Perhaps a new cereal is so good that everybody wants it. Or a record may have such a good sound that many thousands of people want to own it. Stores all over the country may be crowded with people wanting to buy these things.

When many people buy the same thing at the same time, we say there is a big **demand** for that product. You probably want many things you do not buy. Only when you actually buy something do you create a demand for it.

demand
when many people buy a certain good or service

When many people want a certain good, then there is a demand for that good. Here there is a demand for fruit and vegetables.

Who fills the demand for a product? In other words, who makes the things you and many other people spend money to buy? Goods are made by producers. In the case of the cereal, the producer is the company that made the cereal. You will find the company's name printed on the box. In the case of a tape, the producer is the recording company that made the tape for sale.

Producers make things for one main reason. They want to make a profit. Producers must make things consumers are willing to buy. If people do not buy what a producer makes, one of two things will happen. Either the producer will stop making that thing, or the producer will go out of business.

How can consumers tell producers what to make? They tell them by making purchases in the market. A market is a place for buying and selling goods and services. In a free enterprise system such as we have in the United States, all our stores and businesses make up the market. When you the consumer buy something in a store, you tell producers they are making a product you want at a price you are willing to pay. If you do not buy something, you tell producers you do not want that product at that price. In this way consumers affect what producers make.

The owner of this apple juice factory makes apple juice in order to earn a profit.

A producer sells goods at the price that consumers will buy them.

The Law of Demand

Suppose you want something, but you think the price is too high. If a great many other people also feel the price is too high, the store will not sell many of those items. The demand for that item will be low. But what might happen if the store lowered the price? How would demand be affected if the store ran ads on television saying they would sell the item at half the former cost? You and many others may buy the product at the lower price. If you do, then the demand would go up.

The law of demand says that as the price of an item goes up, people will buy less. The law also says that as the price of an item goes down, people will buy more.

The Law of Supply

Producers want to supply what buyers demand. You will remember that the reason they do this is to make a profit. Naturally, sellers want to make the largest profit they can. They do this by charging the highest price that people are willing to pay. When people are willing to buy at a high price, the producer will make more items. The lower the price people are willing to pay, the fewer items the producer will be willing to make. This is called the law of supply.

Putting the laws of supply and demand together, we can say that as the price of something rises, sellers will offer more and buyers will demand less. As the price of a good or service falls, sellers will offer less, and buyers will demand more. This is the law of supply and demand. This law simply sums up what the law of supply and the law of demand say.

The Market Clearing Price

Since producers want to charge the highest price possible, and consumers want to pay the least they can, how are prices set? The market is the place this happens in a free enterprise system. At some price, consumers will buy all that producers are willing to sell. This is called the **market clearing price**. At the market clearing price, supply and demand are equal. Producers will sell what consumers will buy, and no more. Consumers will buy what producers will sell, and no more.

For example, suppose a business makes sweaters that they would like to sell for $40 each. At that price, the business will make, say, ten thousand sweaters. However, they find that consumers will buy only five thousand sweaters at that price. The company finds that consumers will buy twenty thousand sweaters at $20 each. But this price is less than the company is willing to sell the sweaters for. What will be the market clearing price, the price consumers are willing to pay and producers are willing to accept?

Look at the graph below. Look at the solid line labeled supply. It shows that at $60 each, the company will supply twenty thousand sweaters. At $50 it will make fifteen thousand. At $40 each, it will supply ten thousand. At $30

market clearing price
the price at which all of a certain good will be sold

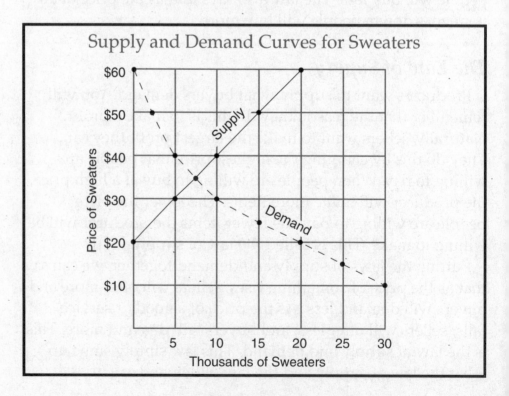

Supply and Demand Curves for Sweaters

The price of this car went down because no one would buy it at the original price. In this way, the producer meets the market clearing price.

each, the company will make only five thousand sweaters. And at $20 each, the company will not supply any sweaters because it cannot make a profit.

Now look at the dotted curved line labeled demand on the graph. It shows that at $60 each, consumers will not buy any of the sweaters. At $50 each, only twenty-five hundred sweaters will be sold. At $10 per sweater, consumers would buy thirty thousand.

Find the place where the solid line and the dotted line cross. This place marks the point at which supply and demand would be equal. At a price of $35 each, consumers would buy exactly as many sweaters as the maker would be willing to produce at that price — 7500 sweaters. Supply and demand would be equal. We say that in this case, $35 would be the market clearing price.

When consumers want to buy more than producers are willing to make, there is a **shortage**. When producers supply more than consumers will buy, there is a **surplus**. By using the market system to find the market clearing price, surpluses and shortages are avoided.

shortage
not enough

surplus
more than enough

The Circular Flow Model of the Economy

There are really two markets operating at the same time in a free enterprise system. We call one market the **resource market**. The other market is the **product market**.

In the resource market, people sell their labor or the things they produce to businesses. For example, a worker in a factory sells his or her time to the factory owner. A farmer sells crops. A miner sells coal, gold, or oil.

In the product market, businesses sell goods or services to consumers. Car companies sell cars. The telephone company sells telephone service. Doctors sell medical care.

The resource and product markets work together to make up the whole economy. Let's say you work at a fast-food place. You are paid money. You spend this money to buy things you need. Today you may need to buy a new pair of shoes. The store takes part of the money you paid for the shoes and pays its workers. Part of the money goes to the company that made the shoes. The company uses part of the money to pay its workers and part of it to pay for the leather in the shoes.

The next time you wait on a customer at work, you may see some of your money again. The worker at the shoe store may come into your fast-food place to buy lunch. Or the person

resource market
where goods and services are sold to producers

product market
where goods and services are sold to consumers

These workers may spend the money they earn on a good made by someone else.

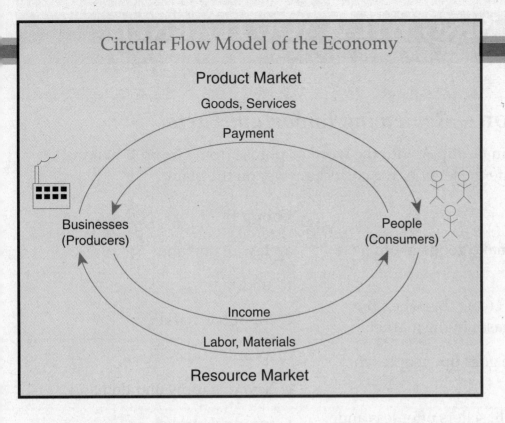

Circular Flow Model of the Economy

Product Market

Goods, Services

Payment

Businesses
(Producers)

People
(Consumers)

Income

Labor, Materials

Resource Market

who made the shoes you bought may stop by for a sandwich. Part of the money they spend may be the same money you paid for your new shoes. You will get part of that money again in your next paycheck. Money flows from people to businesses and back again.

We call this process the circular flow model of the economy. It can be shown as a diagram. Look at the diagram above. The top part of the diagram shows the product market. It shows that businesses sell products to people. People pay money to the businesses for these products. The bottom part of the diagram shows the resource market. People sell resources such as labor and materials to businesses. Businesses pay money to the people for these resources. The money the businesses use is the money people paid for the businesses' products. The resources, products, and money flow in the directions shown by the arrows.

As the circular flow model of the economy shows, the flow of money among businesses and people never stops. Workers depend on businesses for jobs. Businesses depend on workers to buy products. This model shows how the free enterprise system of the United States works.

Comprehension – *Reviewing Important Facts*

Match the sentence in **Group A** with the word or phrase from **Group B** that the sentence explains. Write the letter of the correct answer on the blank.

Group A

_____ 1. Producers make goods in order to get this.

_____ 2. Consumers create this when they make purchases in the market.

_____ 3. As the price goes up, people will buy less.

_____ 4. As prices fall, sellers offer less and people demand more.

_____ 5. Supply and demand are equal.

_____ 6. People want to buy more than suppliers will make.

_____ 7. Workers buy products from producers.

_____ 8. Businesses pay money to people for resources.

Group B

a. law of demand

b. shortage

c. resource market

d. profit

e. law of supply and demand

f. product market

g. demand

h. market clearing price

Vocabulary – *Match Up*

Choose a word or phrase in the box to complete each sentence. Write that word or phrase on the blank.

| surplus | circular flow model | resource market |
| law of supply | product market | market clearing price |

1. If people are willing to pay a high price for an item, the _____ says that producers will make more of that item.

2. The price at which consumers will buy all that producers will make is

the _____ .

3. When producers make more than consumers will buy, there

is a _____ .

4. Farmers sell their crops in the _____ .

5. You buy your food in the _____ .

6. How money gets from consumers to businesses and back to consumers is explained

by the _____ of the economy.

Critical Thinking — *Distinguishing Relevant Information*

Information that is **relevant** is information that is important to what you say or write. Information that does not contribute to what you say or write is not relevant.

Imagine that you have to tell a friend how the circular flow model of the economy operates. Read each sentence below. Decide which sentences are relevant to what you will say. Put a check in front of the relevant sentences.

_____ 1. Two markets operate at the same time in a free enterprise system.

_____ 2. At some price, supply and demand will be equal.

_____ 3. People sell their labor and the things they produce to businesses.

_____ 4. The money you earn at a job buys goods and services from producers.

_____ 5. Businesses sell products to consumers.

_____ 6. Businesses use the money they earn from the sale of their products to pay workers and buy resources.

_____ 7. If people are not willing to pay the price producers charge, there will be a surplus.

_____ 8. The money you spend comes back to you sooner or later.

Comparing Line Graphs

The line graphs below show how much oil was produced and how much was used in the United States per day from 1960 to 1990. Study the graphs. Then answer the questions.

United States Oil Production, 1960 – 1990   United States Oil Usage, 1960 – 1990

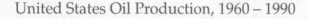

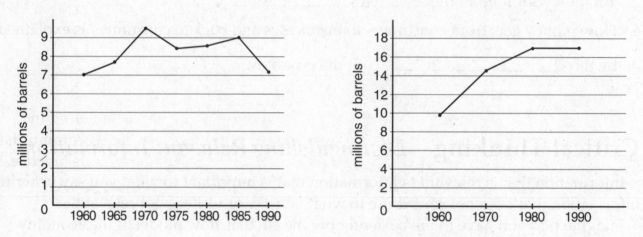

1. About how many millions of barrels of oil did the United States produce per day in 1960? _____

2. About how many millions of barrels of oil did the United States produce per day in 1990? _____

3. How did the United States oil production change between 1960 and 1990?

   _____

4. About how many millions of barrels of oil did the United States use per day in 1960?

   _____

5. About how many millions of barrels of oil did the United States use per day in 1990?

   _____

6. What was the trend in United States oil usage between 1960 and 1990?

   _____

7. Look at your answers to questions 3 and 6. Were the United States oil production and oil usage in balance? What conclusion can you draw?

   _____

SOCIALISM and COMMUNISM

CHAPTER 5

socialism
an economic system where the government provides many programs to all people

communism
an economic system where the government controls the production of goods and services

---

Consider as you read

- What kinds of economy are socialism and communism?
- Where are socialism and communism practiced?

Capitalism is one kind of economy that is practiced in many countries around the world. **Socialism** and **communism** are two other kinds of economies that some nations practice.

Communism is a kind of command economy. In a command economy, the government owns the businesses. The government decides what factories will make. It decides where people will work and how much they will be paid. It decides what farmers will grow. It tells farmers and factories how much they must produce. It sets prices for goods. In communism, the government owns almost all businesses. The people who are not in the government have little say in how the economy is run.

Socialism is a mixed economy. Remember that capitalism is also a mixed economy. But capitalism and socialism are not

This train in France is owned and run by the French government.

Karl Marx

the same. In socialism, the government owns some of the major businesses in the country. However, people not in the government make many economic decisions.

The Ideas of Karl Marx

Both socialism and communism came from the ideas of Karl Marx. Marx lived in Germany over one hundred years ago. Large factories were just coming into use. Workers were treated badly and were not paid well. If they were hurt on the job, they were fired.

Marx thought that workers and owners could not get along with each other. He thought that workers would have to run the factories to make their lives better. Factory owners would not give up without a fight. Marx said that workers should use force to take over.

If workers took over, socialism would result. Everyone would own part of the country's businesses. All people would share wealth. There would be few rich or poor people.

The process would not stop there, according to Marx. As time went on, workers would own more and more businesses. Soon, all people would be both workers and owners. There would be no more private property. The people would own everything together. Since workers and owners would no longer be fighting each other, there would be little for government to do. After a while, government would disappear. This stage would be called communism.

When Marx was young, he saw that the owners of factories treated their workers very poorly.

This farm is owned by the workers, but it is run by the government.

No country today practices socialism or communism exactly as Marx imagined them. However, many countries in the world practice some form of socialism or communism.

Socialism Today

In many countries today, the **public** owns some industries. The public is the people acting together through the government. Public ownership of some industries is a key part of socialism.

People who believe in socialism are called socialists. Socialists believe that public ownership protects workers from bad working conditions and low pay. They think that government must control business. It must tell business what to produce, how to produce it, and to whom to provide it. In this way, the government can see that no one becomes too rich or too poor.

Under socialism, people can work at whatever job they choose. They can own a business. People can own private property.

However, under socialism the government plays a very big part in the economy. First, the government owns some of the very large industries. Health care is one of these industries. Doctors work for the government. Medical care may be free to everyone. The government may also own all the banks. It may own the railroads. It owns all or most of the mines that produce things such as coal, oil, and metals.

public
the people, as opposed to the government

Second, the government plans how the country's resources will be used. It may decide how many cars or houses will be built. It may decide how much steel will be made. The government directs the economy.

Denmark, France, and Sweden are socialist countries. In Sweden the government owns the factories that make steel and ships. It owns the telephone company. It owns parts of such businesses as railroads. The government works with private business to make economic plans for the whole country.

People in Sweden get many things from the government. Medical care is free. So is education through college. Old people or people out of work are cared for. Child care is free. In order for the government to provide these services, the people pay taxes to the government. The tax money is then used to pay for medical care, education, and other programs. Taxes in Sweden are very high. People pay about half their income in taxes.

Communism Today

Under communism, the government owns almost everything. People can own very small farms or businesses. But they must follow rules set by the leaders. People are told where to work. Pay is set by the government.

The Swedish government pays for education, so all children are able to go to school.

Today, people in China may choose to spend money on a new refrigerator. However, very few Chinese can afford one.

The People's Republic of China has more people than any other country. These people live under communism. The government still directs the economy. But China has a limited market system, too. Farmers can rent land from the government. They pay part of their crop as rent. They can sell the rest for profit. People can use their profits to buy animals or equipment.

Factories have changed, too. The government still tells factories what and how much to make. But the people who run the factories can decide how to make the goods. They can sell some goods for profit.

Fewer people live under communism today than did five years ago. Communism is weakening very fast. In 1989, many nations began to turn from communism. It will take time for these nations to have economies that work smoothly. But many people in these nations feel that the change will be worth it.

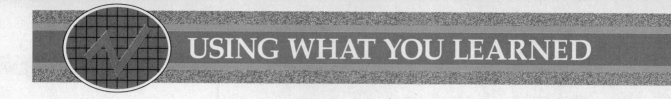

Comprehension — *Matching*

Read each statement. Then look in the box for the economic system it describes. Write the name of the economic system you choose on the blank after each sentence. You will use each name more than once.

socialism	communism

1. The government owns almost all businesses and property. _____

2. People still make many economic decisions. _____

3. There is supposed to be no more need for government. _____

4. The public owns some but not all industries. _____

5. People can own private property. _____

6. People can own only very small farms or businesses. _____

7. The government tells people where to work. _____

8. The government owns some large industries such as health care and

   the railroads. _____

Vocabulary — *Write a Paragraph*

Use six or more words or phrases in the box to write a paragraph that tells about Karl Marx's ideas.

socialism	private property	Germany	large factories
workers	government	communism	force

_____

_____

_____

_____

_____

_____

_____

_____

Critical Thinking — *Cause and Effect*

A **cause** is something that makes something else happen. What happens is called the **effect**.

> **Cause**: There is a scarcity of resources.
> **Effect**: People cannot have everything they want.

Choose a cause or an effect from **Group B** to complete each sentence in **Group A**. Write the letter of the correct answer on the blank. The first one is done for you.

Group A

1. __b__ , so Karl Marx thought that workers and owners could not get along with each other.

2. Factory owners would not give up without a fight, so _____ .

3. In socialism all people would share wealth, so _____ .

4. _____ , so after a while government would disappear.

5. Sweden provides many services for its people, so _____ .

6. _____ , so some people can rent land and make a profit from their crops.

Group B

a. There would be few rich or poor people.

b. Large factories often treated workers badly.

c. China also has a limited market system.

d. There would be little for government to do.

e. Taxes are very high in Sweden.

f. Marx said workers should use force to take over.

Communism Collapses in Eastern Europe and the Former Soviet Union

For 28 years the Berlin Wall divided one of Germany's largest cities. On one side were the East Germans. Ruled by a communist government, they suffered from a lack of the most basic consumer goods. On the other side of the wall were the West Germans. Their democratic government and market economy brought times of plenty. East German soldiers guarded the wall. People from East Germany were not allowed to cross. They were prisoners in their own country.

In just a few days in the fall of 1989, the wall came tumbling down. East Germans had long been fed up with communism. In October they took to the streets demanding change. In early November the government gave in. The Berlin Wall was thrown open. Within months East and West Germany were one country again.

The failure of communism began in the former Soviet Union. By the end of 1991, the former Soviet Union had disintegrated into fifteen independent republics, most of which were moving toward free enterprise. After 75 years, communism had proved to be a dismal failure in the country where it began.

The basic problem with communism was that it never delivered the goods it promised. Most labor and raw materials were used to produce planes, ships, and tanks. The government controlled the entire economy and did so poorly. People worked for low wages. There were few things to buy. People had to stand in line for hours each day just to buy food. One joke in Russia tells about a woman who asks a store clerk, "Doesn't this store have meat?" "No, this is the store that doesn't have eggs," the clerk said. "The store that doesn't have meat is across the street."

In 1990, people in Albania spoke out against the communist government there.

Government control of the means of production was to blame for the problems. A government worker in Moscow, not farmers, decided when crops should be harvested. Often the crops were harvested at the wrong time. Some were gathered before they were ready. Others were gathered too late. About a third of the country's crops rotted in the fields or fell from trucks and trains and was lost.

Soviet leaders knew they had to provide more consumer goods or face revolt. However, it was not easy to change an economic system that had been in place longer than most people had been alive. Soon people grew tired of waiting for change. They took over control of their government and removed the communists from power. Within days the Soviet Union was no longer a country.

The people of Eastern Europe and the former Soviet Union have seen communism fail. "There's a glint in the eyes of the young," said one man. "This gives me hope." The hope is for the future. The hope is for a free market economy.

◆

Write About It

On a separate sheet of paper, write a paragraph that compares the way you live with the way people live under communism.

In the fall of 1989, the Berlin Wall, which had been standing for 28 years, came down.

UNIT 3

AMERICA and FREE ENTERPRISE

America is a land with many "rags to riches" stories. This country is a place where anyone, no matter how rich or how poor, has a chance to succeed by working hard. American history is full of such stories. Andrew Carnegie came to the United States from Scotland. His first job paid $1.20 a week. Carnegie worked, saved, and planned. Later in life he owned a giant steel company and became one of the richest men in the world. He gave away much of his money to libraries.

Carnegie's story has been repeated on a smaller scale millions of times. Each person in America is free to use his or her talents in many ways. Each person can also use his or her resources, money, or labor in many ways. The free enterprise system is based on each person's right to make choices and to benefit or suffer from the results.

Anyone in this country can start a business. People can own a business by themselves or with another person. People can also invest money in the businesses that other people have started. When people go into business, they are taking a risk. They do not know at the beginning whether their business will be a success. But many people feel the rewards are worth the risk. Andrew Carnegie was one of those people.

As we each try to do what we think is best for us, we play our part in making this great economic system work.

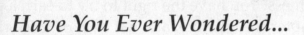

Have You Ever Wondered...

- What are your rights in a free enterprise system?
- What does an entrepreneur do?
- Why are some businesses small while others are large?
- What do labor unions do for workers?
- How does discrimination hurt everyone in the country?

All of these questions will be answered in this unit. You will learn about the key features of the American free enterprise system. You will learn about the important part that entrepreneurs play in free enterprise. You will learn why some people prefer to work alone, while others share business responsibilities. You will read about the most important people in any business, the workers, and how workers band together to protect their rights.

AMERICAN FREE ENTERPRISE

CHAPTER 6

Consider as you read

- How does free enterprise work?
- What rights do consumers and producers in a free enterprise system have?

You live in the American free enterprise system. You have read that in a free enterprise system, the people make most economic decisions. They do this through the market system. But what does this mean to you? How does this affect the way you live?

You have certain economic rights under free enterprise. You have the right to buy and own property. You have the right to make choices based on what is best for you. You have the right to run a business. You have the right to try to earn a profit.

In this chapter we will look at what each of these rights means to you.

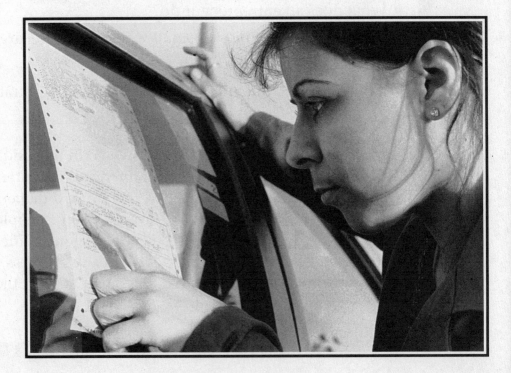

The sticker on this car lets the buyer know whether the car will meet her needs.

The Right To Own Property and Make Contracts

Take a walk in your mind. Walk down a street with houses. Turn and pass by a shopping center. Look in the windows at all the goods. Kick the tires of the cars at an auto dealer.

Everything you have seen is private property. It is owned by someone. That someone may be a person. It may be a business. But each thing has been sold by someone to someone else, perhaps more than once.

Cars, houses, furniture, clothes, and bicycles are all examples of private property. If you have the money, you can buy any of them. Once you have something, you have the right to sell it. No one can tell you how much to charge. You can set any price you wish. Of course, you have to find someone willing to pay that price.

The right to own private property is very important in free enterprise. Think about yourself. You may have a job or hope to get one. Why do you want a job? To make money, of course. But why do you want money? To buy things. The things you buy become your private property. The desire to own property is the real reason you want to work and make money.

Once you buy something and pay for it, it is yours. You and the seller have made an agreement. This agreement is a type of **contract**. Both sides have to follow the contract. If it is not followed by both sides, a court can decide what must be done about breaking the contract.

contract
an agreement between people

Many contracts are in writing. For example, when you buy a house or a car, you and the seller sign a contract. The seller agrees to give you control of the item. You agree to pay for it. You agree that if you cannot pay for it, the seller can take it back. This is a written contract.

Some contracts are not written. These are called oral contracts. Someone you know may hire you to do a job for them. They agree to pay you. If the person does not pay, they have broken the contract. You can ask a court to make them pay.

You can make contracts about many things. The important thing is to know what you agree to in a contract. You are required by law to do what you say you will. You cannot change your mind later and get out of the contract.

The Right To Make Choices That Are Best for You

When you have lunch, you make choices. When you decide what movie to see, you make a choice. When you buy clothes, you make choices.

People who sell goods and services also make choices. A person who sells a car chooses to sell it at some price. A person who takes a job chooses to work for some wage. In a free enterprise system, people are free to make these choices.

All of us, making all these choices, make up the invisible hand that Adam Smith wrote about. We each act in our own self-interest. We each try to do what is best for us. We each have the right to "Look out for number one." Taken all together, our choices are a powerful force in the economy.

Record sales are a good example of the power our choices have. A new musical group makes a record. If many people buy it, the record company will make good profits. They will ask the group to make another record. If the records keep

This man is signing a contract.

In free enterprise people have the right to start their own business.

selling, the group will become famous. The group and the record company may become very rich.

Auto sales also show how important choices are. Gasoline became more costly in the 1970s. People began to buy small cars that used less gas. Since American auto makers did not want to make small cars, Americans bought cars from Japan. American auto makers lost money. So they began to make small cars.

People making choices have changed the United States. Many years ago most people chose to be farmers. Today few people choose to be farmers. Most people choose to work at a job in a city. That is why most people in the United States today live in cities. The right to make choices in a free enterprise system made this change possible.

The Right To Run a Business

You do not have to work for someone else. You can start any business you like. Of course, you cannot break laws. You cannot go into business robbing banks. But you can start a business offering any good or service that is not against the law. Many new businesses are started each year. Some are like other businesses. They offer the same goods or services. Others offer new goods or services.

Each business decides how to run itself. A store decides what to sell. It decides how much to charge. It decides when to have sales. Factories decide what to make and how many to make. They set prices for the goods they make.

Suppose you want to start a business. You decide you will sell hand-painted T-shirts. Since they are a lot of trouble to make, you will charge $50 for each one. After a week you haven't sold any T-shirts. But another store across the street is selling dozens of shirts for $15 each. You have to make a choice. Because of competition from the other store, your business is losing money. You must lower your price or go out of business.

No one can force you to lower your price. But no one can force people to pay your price either. You have the right to run your business the way you want to. But in a free enterprise system, you not only have the right to succeed. You also have the right to fail.

The Right To Earn a Profit

Self-interest drives the market system. We would rather buy goods at low prices than at high prices. We would rather work at jobs that pay well. Businesses would rather sell at high prices than at low prices. Each person and each business tries to earn a profit. In a free enterprise system, this is our right.

The desire to earn profits makes a free enterprise system grow. This is good for all of us, consumers and producers alike. For example, suppose a business wants to make more profits. One way is to sell more goods. To sell more, the business must make its goods better or cheaper than the goods everyone else makes. Either way both the consumer and the producer win.

A business must sometimes lower the price of goods in order to sell them.

Let's say a business makes can openers. It finds a way to make its can openers last longer than any other can openers. Consumers buy a great many of the new can openers. Because sales are so high, the company is able to lower its price and still make good profits. It makes less profit on each can opener. But it sells so many that its total profits increase. The consumer gets a better product at a lower price. And the company makes more money.

But wait. It gets better. Other companies see what is happening. They improve their can openers and lower their prices. Now they have a better can opener at a lower price. They sell more and make bigger profits. So the first company improves its can opener and lowers its prices again.

The competition among producers means that consumers keep getting better products at lower prices. And the reason the producers compete is to make profits. Without profits businesses would have no reason to make better, cheaper products. You would have far fewer choices of things to buy. Many things you did buy would not be very good. And prices would probably be higher. Because businesses want to make profits, they are always looking for ways to give you a better deal. This is the best way they have to get your business.

The Right To Be Free of Government Controls

If you decide to move to another state, you do it. You can change jobs. You can go into or out of business. You can buy and sell property. You can do all this on your own. You do not have to get government permission.

The government does have some say over business. There are laws that we all must follow. Some of these laws help control the economy. For example, a law sets a minimum wage, the lowest amount an employer can pay its workers. Since labor costs affect prices, this law means we may pay more for some things. However, it also protects workers.

Free enterprise means the right to do business without government control. But it does not mean a business can do things that would hurt others. The government is like a referee in a football game. The government makes sure that everyone follows the rules. You will learn more about government and the economy in Unit 5.

Comprehension — *Reviewing Important Facts*

Match the sentence in **Group A** with the phrase from **Group B** that shows your economic right under free enterprise. Write the letter of the correct answer on the blank.

Group A

_____ 1. You decide to buy a new water heater that uses less electricity than your old one.

_____ 2. The price of raw materials goes up, so a business raises its prices in order to keep making the same amount of money.

_____ 3. You decide to move to another state to take a job, and you ask no one's permission.

_____ 4. You sign a paper agreeing to sell your house.

_____ 5. You have a sign in your store that says "No shirt, no shoes, no service."

Group B

a. the right to be free of government controls

b. the right to run a business

c. the right to make choices that are best for you

d. the right to own property and make contracts

e. the right to earn a profit

Vocabulary — *Writing With Vocabulary Words*

Use six or more words in the box to write a paragraph that tells what your economic rights in a free enterprise system mean to you.

goods and services	self-interest	competition	profit
private property	choices	government	contract

_____

_____

_____

_____

_____

_____

_____

_____

_____

Critical Thinking – *Categories*

Read the words in each group. Decide how they are alike. Write a title for each group on the blank beside each group. You may use the words in the box for all or part of each title.

contract	business	property	choices	profit

1. buying clothes
   taking a job
   self-interest   _____

2. desire to make money
   better products at lower prices
   competition   _____

3. buying and selling things
   desire for wealth
   better life   _____

4. seller
   buyer
   written or oral agreement   _____

5. offer goods or services
   sales
   competition   _____

CHAPTER 7

Consider as you read

- How do businesses get started?
- How are businesses run?

You have read how land, labor, and capital work together to produce goods and services. You also read that people are needed to make these factors of production work together. People are needed to take raw materials and use labor and machines to make products. People are needed to provide services.

Some people work alone to provide goods or services. Other people work together. Some businesses have only one or two workers. Others have thousands. But no matter what their size, all businesses started in the same way. They started with one person who had an idea for a way to make money.

Michael Dell, a successful entrepreneur, started his own computer factory.

In a sole proprietorship, one person owns and runs the business.

The Entrepreneur

Have you ever played with a Frisbee? Have you ever used a Macintosh computer? Have you ever ridden in a Ford automobile? How are all these alike?

The Frisbee, Ford, and Macintosh are all alike in this way. Each is made by a business that was started by one person. That person had an idea. That person also wanted to make money. In each case, the person started a business. The person used land, labor, and capital to make a certain good.

A person who sets up a business to make a profit is an **entrepreneur**. College students used lids from Mother Frisbie's cookie jars to play a game. But that's all it was — a game. Then an entrepreneur took the idea for this new toy and started a business making Frisbees. Today Frisbees are flown in countries all over the world. The entrepreneur made a great deal of money.

entrepreneur
the person who takes an idea and turns it into a product

Of course, not every new business makes money. Many fail. When that happens, the entrepreneur loses money. There is a large **risk** in starting a new business. Many entrepreneurs have lost all they had when their businesses failed. Why do entrepreneurs take the risk? They know that if the business does well, they will make a profit. Sometimes these profits can be very large. The hope of making a lot of money makes the risk seem worthwhile.

risk
the danger that something bad will happen

People who start businesses have choices to make. They must decide whether to work alone or with other people. Each way has its good and bad points.

Sole Proprietorships

sole proprietorship
a business owned by one person

A **sole proprietorship** is a kind of business that is easy to start. A person who wants to make wooden toys, for example, can just start working. Often, little money is needed to get the business going. A sole proprietor gets to keep all the money the business makes. And there is no one to tell the person what to do. Many people like being their own boss.

There are some bad things about being a sole proprietor. The risk is great. If the business fails, the person loses all the money put into the business. Also, there is often no one to help run the business. The sole proprietor has to do many different jobs. The person has to make all the goods or provide all the services. He or she must also do the banking, keep records, order materials, and sell the good or service. Sole proprietors often work long hours.

Sole proprietorships are the most common kind of business in the United States. About seven out of ten businesses are owned by one person. Your doctor, baker, and service-station owner are probably sole proprietors.

Partnerships

partnership
a business owned by two or more people

Sometimes people work together in a business. About one business in ten in the United States is a **partnership**.

Business Ownership

Sole Proprietorship	Partnership	Corporation
Owner/Manager	Owners/Managers	Owners/Stockholders
Workers	Workers	Managers
		Workers

Partnerships let people share work and expenses. Two auto mechanics may decide to set up a repair shop together. Instead of needing to rent two buildings, they need only one. One person may be better at working on engines. The other may be better at working on brakes. Each can do the work he or she does best. And they can share the other work of running a business.

Like sole proprietorships, partnerships are easy to set up. They do not take a lot of money to form. The partners have someone to talk over problems with. Risks are shared. If the business loses money, the partners share the loss. Each person loses less money.

There are some problems with partnerships. It is important for the partners to have a contract with each other. The contract should say who will do what work. It should say how the profits will be shared. Otherwise the partners may argue about these things. This can hurt the business.

Partners can still argue about things. Two people just may not get along. Or they may argue about how to run the business. One person may think the business should borrow a lot of money and grow quickly. The other person may want the business to "pay as it goes," or not borrow money, and grow slowly. Arguments between partners can mean work does not get done.

If the business does borrow money, both partners owe the money. If one partner dies or will not pay, the other has to pay all the debt. Each person has to risk his or her own money. If the business fails, the money can be lost.

Partners share the risk and profits of a business.

Corporations

A **corporation** is another kind of business. It is owned by **stockholders**. Stockholders do not take part in running the business. They put their money into the business by buying shares of **stock**. A stockholder owns part of a company.

By law, a corporation is treated as if it were a person. It can borrow money. It can buy land. It can buy buildings. It can hire and fire workers. About two businesses in ten in the United States are corporations.

Corporations solve many of the problems caused when one or two people own a business. The owners do not run a

corporation
a business owned by many people

stockholders
persons who own part of a company

stock
the part of a company that a person owns

Corporate Managers

corporation on a daily basis. However, they are involved in making important decisions for the business. Other people are hired to manage the business and do the work. People who can do each kind of job well can be hired. This can make a corporation very efficient. Being efficient means doing the most amount of work with the least amount of effort or expense. A business that is efficient can make better products at lower cost. This increases profits.

If a corporation fails, the owners lose only the money they paid for their stock. If the business cannot pay back borrowed money, the owners do not have to pay. However, if the business makes money, the stockholders share in the profits.

Corporations have some problems. Because corporations are usually large businesses, it takes a lot of money to start one. Sometimes it can take a long time for decisions to be made. The business may lose money while people are deciding what to do. Corporations also pay high taxes. Some people say corporations are taxed twice. The business pays taxes on its profits. Then it sends the profits left to the stockholders. The stockholders must then pay taxes on the money they make.

Competition Among Businesses

No matter how a business is organized, most must compete with other businesses. Take a trip down a street in your neighborhood. How many stores sell the same kinds of things? All these stores compete for your business. In some cases, however, just one business controls the entire market. How many electric power companies can you choose from? In most places, the answer is just one.

perfect competition
a market in which no one controls the prices

In **perfect competition**, there are many buyers and sellers. No one buyer or seller controls prices. The goods or services offered by the different sellers are just alike. Buyers find it easy to learn about the products and compare prices. The cost of starting such a business is low.

There is no perfect competition in the United States today. Some businesses always grow larger than others. These large businesses are able to affect the prices people pay. They can lower prices and drive other companies out of business. Then they can raise prices again.

Having a choice among many businesses that provide the same good or service is part of the free enterprise system.

A **monopoly** is the opposite of perfect competition. Electric power companies are monopolies. You have no choice of companies to buy electricity from. Only one set of wires comes to your house. You must buy electricity from the company that owns those wires.

You might think that a monopoly would charge very high prices. That is not necessarily true. It would be very costly for more than one electric company to string wires to every house. This would make the cost of electricity very high. The government gives just one company the right to sell electricity in an area. To protect consumers, it limits the price the company can charge.

Sometimes a few very large companies control an **industry**. In some **oligopolies**, the products of all companies are the same. There is little difference in oil or steel. Oil from Texas or oil from Ohio can both be made into gasoline. You can't tell if the steel in a knife is from one maker or another.

The auto industry in the United States is one oligopoly. Although there are differences among the cars, there are only a few companies that make them.

An oligopoly often results when it is very costly to get into a business. It costs a great deal of money to build a factory to make cars or television sets. Billions of dollars may have to be spent before the first sale is made. This limits the number of people who get into the business.

monopoly
a market in which there is only one seller of a product

industry
the making of a certain good or service; for example, the oil industry

oligopolies
only a few companies providing a good or service

Providing electricity is an example of a monopoly in the United States.

An oligopoly has some control over prices. However, competition protects consumers. If one oil company charges too much for gasoline, people will buy from other companies. It is against the law for companies to agree on what the price of a certain good will be. In this way competition keeps prices down.

Entrepreneurs take risks and start companies to provide many kinds of goods and services. Companies are organized in different ways. But all companies depend on workers. In the next chapter, you will read about the most important people in a company — the workers.

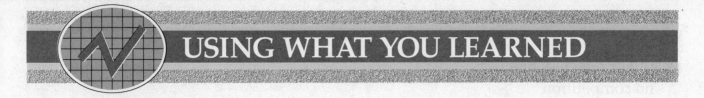

Comprehension — *Matching*

Read each statement. Then look in the box for the kind of business it tells about. Write the name of the kind of business on the blank after each sentence.

sole proprietorship	partnership	corporation
monopoly	oligopoly	

1. "It's nice to have someone with whom to share the work and the problems."

   _____

2. "There are only a few other companies that make the goods we make."

   _____

3. "Since there is no one to help me do the many different things I have to do, I work a

   lot of long hours." _____

4. "If you want it, you've got to buy it from me."

   _____

5. "I own part of the company, but I don't have to do any of the work."

   _____

Vocabulary — *Exclusions*

One word or phrase in each group does not belong. Find that word and cross it out. Then write a sentence that tells how the other words are alike.

1. turns an idea into a product _____
   takes risks
   stock   _____
   can succeed or fail
                  _____

2. two or more people   _____
   have a contract
   stockholders   _____
   share expenses and profits
                           _____

3. unfair business practices
   no competition
   electric company
   oligopoly

   _____

   _____

   _____

4. one owner
   most common business
   shared risk
   easy to start

   _____

   _____

   _____

5. low taxes
   owned by stockholders
   produces goods and services efficiently
   hires others to work

   _____

   _____

   _____

Critical Thinking — *Fact and Opinion*

Read each sentence below. If the sentence is a fact, write **F** on the blank. If the sentence is an opinion, write **O** on the blank. If the sentence gives both a fact and an opinion, write **FO** on the blank, and circle the part of the sentence that is an opinion.

_____ 1. Entrepreneurs can make a lot of money, but they can also lose a lot.

_____ 2. There is a large risk in starting a new business, but the risk is worth it.

_____ 3. A sole proprietorship is the best kind of business because you are your own boss.

_____ 4. Partnerships let each person do the kind of work he or she is best at.

_____ 5. The best businesses in the United States are corporations.

_____ 6. If you own stock in a corporation that fails, you should never buy stock again.

_____ 7. Electric power companies are an example of a monopoly.

_____ 8. The government controls monopolies, but they would be more efficient without rules.

_____ 9. Gasoline companies are an oligopoly, and that is why prices are so high.

_____ 10. It is against the law for companies to agree on the price of a certain good.

Reading a Stock Market Report

The stock market report below shows information about six different stocks. Study the report. Then answer the questions.

52-week High	Low	Stock	Div.	Sales 100s	High of the Day	Low of the Day	Last of the Day	Chg. in Price
68½	55½	Texaco	3.20	9687	61⅜	60⅛	61	+1½
39⅜	21¼	TmMir	1.08	2034	31½	30⅜	31½	+¾
37½	27⅛	USX	1.40	10934	31⅛	30½	30½	+⅛
44⅝	33	Upjohn	1.16	10578	42¼	41⅜	42	−¼
32	20	Walgrns	.46	4192	32⅞	31½	32⅞	+1¼
24	13¾	Wynns	.60	17	18½	18	18	−½

1. What was the highest price paid for USX stock in the last year?

   _____

2. What was the lowest price paid for Upjohn stock on this day?

   _____

3. Which stock showed the largest change in price from one day to the next?

   _____

4. Which stock shown paid the highest dividend (Div.)?

   _____

5. What dividend was paid by Wynns per share?

   _____

6. If a person owned 1,000 shares of Texaco, how much dividend was that person paid?

   _____

7. How many 100s of shares of Wynns stock were sold?

   _____

LABOR and LABOR UNIONS

CHAPTER 8

◆

Consider as you read

• Why are people in different jobs paid different amounts?

• What are workers' rights?

• How are workers' rights protected?

◆

Talk to the top person in any large company and ask him or her what, more than anything else, makes the company successful. Usually the answer will be the same. "It's the people who make the company successful." The person will say, "We owe everything to the people who work here."

Land, labor, and capital are needed to make a company grow. Why are people the most important? Without people, nothing would get done. Every business depends on labor.

Labor is the most important part of business.

After these women learn to use these machines, they will become part of the labor force.

The Labor Force

Are you part of the labor force? To answer that question, you must answer three other questions. The three questions are: (1) Are you sixteen years old or older? (2) Are you working or looking for work? (3) Are you a **civilian**? If your answer to all three questions is yes, then you are a member of the labor force.

Many people who are younger than sixteen hold jobs. However, they are not counted as part of the labor force. This is because most people of this age are still in school. Some people older than sixteen have no job. They are not looking for work. Perhaps they are retired. They may be sick. Or they may have lost hope of finding a job and stopped looking. These people are not counted as part of the labor force. People who are in the army, navy, or air force are not part of the labor force. They have a job they cannot leave for a period of time. Only people who could take a job if it were offered to them are counted. About half the people in the United States are part of the labor force.

Factors Affecting Income

Not all workers make the same wage. Some people are paid very little. Others get a great deal of money. Several factors affect how much money people make.

civilian
someone who is not in the armed forces

skill
ability to do something

The kind of job a person does has a lot to do with how much the person is paid. Some jobs take more **skill** than others. A person who digs ditches may have few skills. That person needs to know how to pick up dirt with a shovel and not much else. A doctor must have many skills. A doctor needs to know how to tell why people are sick. A doctor must know how to make people well. A doctor has many more skills than a ditch digger. Doctors are paid more than ditch diggers.

Few people are born with all the skills they will ever need. Most people learn their skills while going to school. People go to school to learn all kinds of jobs. Checkers at the food store go to school. Teachers go to school. Doctors and lawyers go to school.

In general, the more education a person has, the more money he or she will make. A person who quits school in the tenth grade will usually make less than a person who graduates. A person who goes to college will usually make more than a person who finishes only high school.

It takes time and money to go to school. Some people would rather go to work as soon as they are old enough. However, going to school can really pay off. Look at the chart on page 79. It shows how much a person can expect to earn based on how many years the person goes to school. A person who has

This woman went to school to learn the skill of writing for a newspaper.

The Relationship of Education to Money Earned

Years of School	Probable Annual Earnings	
	Male	Female
Eight years	$18,946	$12,655
High school graduate	$24,745	$16,223
1–3 years college	$29,253	$19,336
4 years college	$38,117	$23,506
5 or more years college	$47,903	$30,255

five or more years of college can expect to make about twice as much as someone who does not finish high school.

The chart also shows that a man's income is usually much higher than a woman's income. People argue that women are not given the chance to get better-paying jobs. Many women are paid less even if they are doing the same jobs as men. The government is working to make sure that women are treated fairly by employers.

Laws also affect how much money people make. The United States has a minimum-wage law. The minimum wage is the least amount a worker can be paid. Businesses that must pay the minimum wage must have a sign telling what the wage is. Of course, businesses can pay more than the minimum wage. Many do.

Discrimination

Some **discrimination** is legal. For example, you may shop at any store you like. If you run a business, you can hire any person you think will be best able to do a job. You may hire a friend's child. You may hire someone simply because you like them. You may pay one person more than another even though they do the same kind of job. This often happens because one person has been working at the job longer.

discrimination
the act of treating people differently than others

79

Another kind of discrimination lets people do certain things only if they pass a test. Until they pass a test, doctors cannot treat patients. You cannot drive a car until you reach a certain age. This kind of discrimination helps everyone. You would not want to go to a doctor who did not know enough to pass a test. And you would not want to drive on the same street with someone who could not pass a driving test.

Other kinds of discrimination are against the law. In 1964, Congress passed the Civil Rights Act. It is against this law to discriminate against people because of their race, religion, sex, or **national origin**. The Equal Pay Act of 1963 says that women who do the same jobs as men must get the same pay. In 1967, Congress said that people between the ages of 40 and 70 cannot be discriminated against because of their age.

What does this mean to you? It means that when you apply for a job, the employer must consider only you and your ability to do the job. The job can be given to the person the employer feels will do the best job. The person who gets the job may have done similar work before. The person may have more training. But a job cannot be denied to someone just

national origin
the country a person comes from

Places of business must hang this sign.

Members of labor unions gather to speak out for better working conditions.

because they belong to a certain race or religion. A job cannot be denied to a person just because the person is a man or a woman.

Discrimination can still happen. However, it is against the law. The Equal Employment Opportunity Commission works to see that discrimination is corrected.

Labor Unions

Just over a hundred years ago, most people in America worked on farms or in small businesses. Then large factories began. Most people no longer worked alone. People began working with many others.

In a small business, workers know the owner. If their pay is too low, or there is a danger on the job, they can talk to the owner. In very large businesses, workers may not know the owner. This can make it hard to get changes made.

The first large factories did not treat workers well. People worked twelve hours a day, seven days a week. Pay was low. Often people got hurt on the job. They were not taken care of, and they were often fired. When people got too old to work, they were fired.

Workers decided to join together to improve working conditions. They formed groups called **labor unions**. One of the first unions was the Knights of Labor. Any worker could

labor unions
groups of workers who work together to look out for their best interests

81

belong to this union. The Knights of Labor worked an eight-hour day. They wanted to stop child labor. They did not believe children should be made to work in factories.

The Knights of Labor were strong in the 1880s. They held many **strikes** to win rights for workers. When people stop work, products do not get made. This hurts the business. Owners will try to work out problems to avoid strikes.

By 1900, the Knights of Labor was weak. A new union arose. This was the American Federation of Labor (AFL). The AFL was open only to skilled workers. By 1920, it had four million members. It won higher pay and shorter hours for workers. Work places were made safer.

After 1920, business owners got laws passed that hurt unions. Many people were out of work during the Great Depression of the 1930s . This also hurt the AFL. Since there were few jobs, workers could not afford to lose their jobs.

Another labor union was formed during the 1930s. The Congress of Industrial Organizations (CIO) began in 1935 as part of the AFL. The CIO became a separate union in 1937. It was open to almost all workers. In 1955, the AFL and CIO became one union again. Today over 90 smaller unions are

These men started the Knights of Labor.

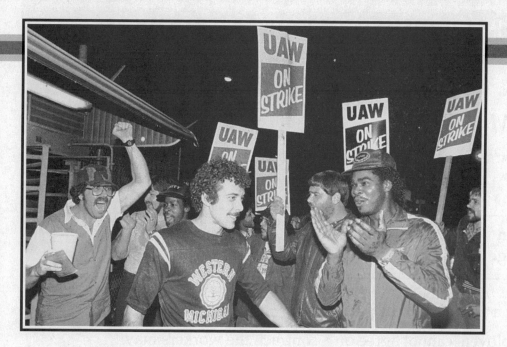

Sometimes unions will go on strike to fight for higher wages or better working conditions.

part of the AFL-CIO. About thirteen million workers belong to the AFL-CIO.

Unions have been a powerful tool for workers. Union workers get higher pay than nonunion workers. Union workers also receive more **fringe benefits**. Sick pay, paid holidays, vacation time, and insurance are some fringe benefits. Some companies share profits with workers.

fringe benefits
things given to workers in addition to their pay

Workers have the right to a clean, safe place in which to work. Unions have helped get safety rules in factories. They have helped get laws passed to make work places safer. For example, laws require safety shields on machine parts that move and could injure someone. Workers who use dangerous chemicals must be told about the dangers. They must be given clothes that protect them.

Unions play a big part in getting contracts for workers. The contracts tell how much workers will be paid. The contracts say in writing what fringe benefits workers will get. The contract is a legal agreement. The company cannot refuse to do what it says.

In 1945, over 35 million Americans belonged to unions. Today fewer than 20 million belong. Fewer people today work in factories. Many companies pay good wages and have good fringe benefits without being forced to. Many people see less need for unions than in the past. More businesses than ever before recognize that workers are the most important part of any business.

Vocabulary — *Match Up*

Choose a word or phrase from the box to complete each sentence. Write that word or phrase on the blank.

discrimination	fringe benefits	labor union	skill
minimum wage	strike	civilian	

1. The lowest amount a worker is to be paid is the _____ .

2. If workers and employers cannot agree on a contract, the workers may

   go on _____ .

3. Refusing to hire a person because of his or her age is _____ .

4. If you are not in the armed forces, you are a _____ .

5. Most people go to school to learn a _____ .

6. Union workers get _____ such as sick pay and insurance.

7. Two examples of a _____ are the Knights of Labor and the AFL-CIO.

Comprehension — *Write the Answer*

Write one or more sentences to answer each question.

1. What three things determine whether a person is part of the labor force? _____

   _____

   _____

2. How do skills affect income? _____

   _____

3. What does the Equal Employment Opportunity Commission do? _____

   _____

4. Describe two kinds of discrimination that are legal. _____

_____

5. What does the Civil Rights Act of 1964 say? _____

_____

6. Why should women know about the Equal Pay Act of 1963? _____

_____

7. Why did workers decide to form labor unions? _____

_____

8. How have labor unions helped workers in America? _____

_____

_____

Critical Thinking – *Drawing Conclusions*

Read the paragraph below and the sentences that follow it. Put a check in front of the conclusions that can be drawn from the paragraph.

> The kind of job a person does has a lot to do with how much the person is paid. Most people learn their skills while going to school. The more education a person has, the more money he or she will make.

_____ 1. Women and men with the same amount of education will make the same amount of money.

_____ 2. Going to school is a way to get better skills.

_____ 3. A person with a lot of education is likely to have a better job than someone with little education.

_____ 4. A person with a college education will make twice as much as someone who does not finish high school.

_____ 5. It is legal to discriminate among people based on their skills and education.

_____ 6. Usually a person with more education gets higher pay than a person with less education.

America's Grand Dame of Mexican Food

"I started with very little money, and I built a nice business that supports 1,000 families. I think that is quite an accomplishment. It is good for the community. It is good for the families. It is good for everyone. I think it's terrific what one woman can do."

—Ninfa Laurenzo, Entrepreneur

If you have enjoyed Mexican foods, such as tacos al carbon, you know why Ninfa Laurenzo is famous. She was the first to make and sell these foods in the United States. But success came slowly. The story of Ninfa Laurenzo is one of hard work.

Ninfa María Rodriguez was born in Harlingen, Texas. As a young woman, she and her Italian husband, Tommy Laurenzo, started a business in Houston. They sold tortillas and pizzas. When Tommy died, Ninfa took over the business.

Government rules soon required Ninfa to buy new equipment to keep the factory open. She decided to open a small restaurant to make more money. She used pots and pans from her own kitchen. Her five children cooked, cleaned, and waited tables. At the end of the first day, they had taken in $170. "We were excited!" says Laurenzo. They had seen that the free enterprise system could work for them.

Only days after the restaurant opened, it caught fire. But Laurenzo refused to quit. "I said to the kids, 'We've got to get in there with soap and water and whatever it takes to redo the place,'" she recalls. But mostly it was Mama Ninfa who made it work. "I'd faint in the kitchen and get up and wash my face and start all over again," she says.

Soon people told their friends about Ninfa's great food. Newspapers wrote about her. Movie stars began to eat at her restaurant. Ninfa's became the place to eat in Houston.

Ninfa Laurenzo

From one restaurant grew others, until Ninfa's included restaurants in several cities. The family that was thrilled to sell $170 worth of food their first day in business built a business that takes in $20 million a year.

Ninfa gives much of the credit to her family and other workers. "I'm the axle, but they are the wheels," she says. "The credit has to go to them."

Still, there would be no Ninfa's without Ninfa. She was determined to succeed. The first time she tried to borrow money from a bank to expand, a banker laughed in her face. "I walked away, got in my car, and cried. But I swore up and down I'd get that money," she says. And get it she did.

"Why have I continued to struggle to make this company a strong one?" she asks. "At first it was about survival and making a living for myself and my five children. But I also don't believe in failing or giving up."

Write About It

On a separate piece of paper, write a paragraph that tells why Ninfa Laurenzo is a successful entrepreneur.

Ninfa Laurenzo runs several Mexican restaurants like this one.

MONEY, BANKING, and INVESTMENT

During its war for independence from England, the young United States printed money that soon became worthless. People found themselves with money that they could not spend. The value of the dollar has gone up and down several times during the history of the United States. One of the biggest problems the United States has faced throughout its history has been providing a supply of money that meets people's needs.

Besides knowing that the value of money will not change, people want other things from their money. What would you do if you only had one-dollar bills? You would have to carry a lot of bills around with you. You could not buy anything for less than one dollar. What if bills were made of paper that could not stand up to a lot of handling? Since money is so important to the economy, it has to be long-lasting.

People don't want to carry their money around with them all the time. So they leave their money in banks. Banking is a big industry in the United States.

Money, perhaps more than anything else, puts Americans in touch with their government. The money in our pockets has value only as long as we have confidence in our government. Our government guarantees that the money we keep in banks is safe. An American president once said, "The business of America is business." He might well have added that the business of business is money.

Have You Ever Wondered...

- What does a bank do with your money?

- Why is it important to save?

- Why does it sometimes make sense to buy on credit?

- How does a check you send to a company in another state come back to you?

- How does the government affect whether you get or lose a job?

In this unit you will learn the answers to these questions. You will read about what a bank does. You will learn why some things are money and others are not. You will learn how and why the United States set up its banking system. You will read about how people manage their money to get the things they want and need. You will learn how your actions and those of your government influence the supply of money.

MONEY and the BANKING SYSTEM

◆ ◆

CHAPTER 9

Consider as you read

- What is money?
- What do banks do?

◆ ◆

money
anything that people take in payment for goods or services

Often when we want something, we can't have it because we don't have the **money** to pay for it. If we borrow money, we have to pay it back. We spend time worrying about money. Sometimes it seems life would be simpler if there were no money.

Actually, money makes our lives better and simpler. This is because money does things for us that nothing else can.

How Money Is Used

Look at a dollar bill or other piece of paper money of the United States. On the front it says, "This note is legal tender for all debts, public and private." This means that stores will take money in payment for the goods they sell. People everywhere will take money in payment for the work they do.

Money makes it much easier to exchange goods and services.

Money is a medium of exchange.

They do this because they know that the money can be spent anywhere else in the United States for other goods or services.

Money is used as a **medium of exchange**. Money is not the only medium of exchange. You can trade goods or services with other people. You might shovel snow from someone's sidewalk in exchange for a sweater. Someone might fix your car for apples from your tree.

Trading things can create problems, though. Two people who trade have to want what the other has. And both have to agree that two items are worth about the same. Can the auto repair shop use your apples? How many apples does it take to pay for a brake job?

Money solves both these problems. Everyone takes money. The owner of the repair shop may not want your apples. But she will accept money because she can use that to buy what she wants.

Money also lets us compare the value of things. We use it as a **standard of value**. The price of a brake job is measured in dollars, not apples.

Suppose you could buy anything you wanted with apples from your tree. You would get apples from the tree once a year. Apples rot within a few months. The older they get, the less they are worth. Money is different. Money can be used as a **store of value**. Diamonds and gold are also often used as stores of value.

medium of exchange
anything that buyers and sellers will both accept

standard of value
something used to measure the worth of different things

store of value
something that will keep its worth over time

Characteristics of Money

Not just anything can be money. What we use for money must be special in several ways.

Look at a dollar bill. Unless it is very new, it may be wrinkled, faded, and a little dirty. The corners may be folded over. People may have written on it. All this tells you that this same dollar bill has been used by many different people. Someday, the bill will be worn out. But it will last for many months or even years. Something we use for money must have **durability**.

When you looked at that dollar bill, where did you get it? It came from someone's pocket or purse. Money is small and light. Money must have **portability**. Think how much trouble it would be to go shopping if dollar bills were as big as blankets and weighed five pounds!

Not everything costs the same. One thing you buy may cost half a dollar. Another may cost fifteen dollars. Yet you can pay for either with a twenty-dollar bill. You can do this because money has **divisibility**. If you pay for a half-dollar item with a twenty-dollar bill, you may be given a ten, a five, four ones, and a fifty-cent piece in change. Divisibility lets you pay exact amounts for anything you buy.

Suppose you did a job for someone last summer. You saved the money for a winter coat. You felt safe about saving the money because you knew it was a store of value. You knew it would keep its value over time. The dollar you earned last summer would still be worth a dollar when winter came. What we use for money must have **stability**.

What Banks Do

A bank is simply a business. Like other businesses, banks try to make a profit. They do this by providing services and charging for those services.

Three common services banks provide are checking accounts, savings accounts, and loans.

Most people have a checking account because it makes it easier and safer to pay bills. A checking account is money a person leaves with a bank until it is needed. When the person

Writing a check

durability
the ability to stand up to wear

portability
the ability to be carried easily

divisibility
the ability to be divided into smaller units

stability
the ability to keep the same value over time

Many people put their money into savings accounts where it will earn interest.

needs to pay a bill, he or she writes an order to the bank. This order is called a check. It tells the bank to pay so much money to the person named on the check.

Having a checking account means you do not have to carry all your money around with you. This keeps your money safe from being lost or stolen. Also, checks can be sent through the mail. A check can be cashed, or turned into money, only by the person to whom it is written. If you send cash through the mail, anyone can take the money. Checks make it easy to send money to people across town or even far away.

Banks also offer savings accounts. People who have more money than they need at the moment can put the extra in a savings account. The bank pays **interest** to people with the savings account. That means that when they get their money back from the bank, there will be more of it.

interest
money paid for the use of other money

The bank uses the money people have in their checking and savings accounts to make loans. Banks lend people money to buy cars, homes, and other things. The bank charges interest on these loans. It charges more interest on loans than it pays on savings accounts. This is how the bank makes a profit.

Money and Banking in the United States

When the United States became a country in 1776, several kinds of money were in use. Some banks had their own money. Gold or silver coins from other countries were used as money. Some people used animal skins or kegs of tobacco.

Some Native Americans used beads. The new United States put out paper money, too.

Having several different kinds of money was confusing. How much was a fox skin worth in gold or beads? Trade between people using different kinds of money was hard. Suppose you wanted to sell a cow, and the person who wanted to buy it had only corn to pay with. Perhaps you did not need any corn. You would then have to find someone else to buy the corn using the kind of money you wanted.

The value of things like skins and corn is not stable. Suppose all farmers were to grow plenty of corn one year. There might be a surplus of corn. The value of corn would go down. If you had a barn full of corn you had been saving, it would be worth less. You would lose.

That barn full of corn could be a problem in other ways. Corn is not durable. Rats can eat it. The roof can leak and ruin it. A barn full of corn is not portable. Corn is heavy and takes up a lot of room.

People faced all these problems in the early United States. They had no single medium of exchange. There were several standards of value. Some of the things used as money lacked durability, portability, or divisibility. Most serious of all the problems, however, was the lack of stability in the money used.

Native Americans and early settlers traded goods. They did not have currency.

These bills were made in Alabama during the Civil War.

While the United States was fighting for its freedom, it printed paper money. This paper money was used to buy arms and pay soldiers. It was used to buy food for the army and all the other things the government needed.

The problem was that the value of this paper money was not stable. People knew that if the United States lost the war, the money would be worthless. As the war went on, the money did become worth less and less. It could not be used as a store of value. This hurt anyone who accepted the money and did not spend it right away. Many people refused to take the money. It could not be used as a medium of exchange.

The United States won its freedom. People remembered the problems they had with money. They wanted stable money. They made providing stable money a main job of the new government.

People wanted the new government to set up a bank to handle the government's money. The bank would keep the government's money safe. It would pay the government's bills. It would check on private banks to be sure they kept people's money safe. It would also put out the money the government made.

In 1791, the government set up the First Bank of the United States. The government also made United States dollars the official money in the country. These two things gave the United States stable money for the first time.

Some people felt the bank had too much power. Finally the bank was closed. This caused many problems. Small banks put out their own money. Sometimes these banks then went out of business. The money became worthless. Many people lost all their money this way. People had to keep a list of bad money. Before they would take money from someone, they had to check the list to see if the money was good. Once again the United States did not have stable money.

In 1863, the government set up a new banking system. Since that time there have been two kinds of banks. National banks must do business under rules set up by the national government. State banks do business under rules set up by state governments. The rules of the national government are strict. Money kept in a national bank is very safe.

Also in 1863, the government decided to use the national banks to issue money that was good anywhere in the United States. Soon small banks stopped putting out their own money. At last the United States had one kind of money that was very stable.

Today most banks in the United States are national banks. They are part of the Federal Reserve System. You will learn more about the Federal Reserve System in Chapter 11.

National banks follow strict rules set by the government.

Comprehension — *Reviewing Important Facts*

Match the sentence in **Group A** with the word or phrase from **Group B** that the sentence explains. Write the letter of the correct answer on the blank.

Group A

_____ 1. Both buyers and sellers will accept money in payment for goods and services.

_____ 2. A dollar bill can be used many times before it is worn out.

_____ 3. The value of money stays about the same from one week to the next.

_____ 4. Price tags on things in stores help us decide whether to spend our money on those things.

_____ 5. Money is made in sizes that fit in our pockets easily.

_____ 6. When we need money from our bank account, we write an order to the bank to pay the money.

_____ 7. Banks pay us to leave money in our savings accounts.

_____ 8. People in the new United States wanted a stable money supply, so the government started this.

_____ 9. These banks issue money that can be used anywhere in the United States.

_____ 10. This is the official money of the United States.

Group B

a. durability

b. standard of value

c. check

d. First Bank of the United States

e. dollar

f. medium of exchange

g. national banks

h. portability

i. interest

j. stability

Vocabulary — *Find the Meaning*

Write the word or phrase that best completes each sentence on the blank.

1. Something that will keep its worth over a period of time can be used

   as a _____ .
   medium of exchange   standard of value   store of value

2. Something that lets us compare the value of different things can be used

   as a _____ .
   medium of exchange   standard of value   store of value

3. The fact that we have coins and bills of different values shows that our money

   has the quality called _____ .
   portability   stability   divisibility

4. Although it is not a good idea, you can bury money in the ground for a long time

   because of its _____ .
   durability   divisibility   portability

5. People feel safe about saving money because of its _____ .
   portability   divisibility   stability

Critical Thinking — *Distinguishing Relevant Information*

Imagine that you have to tell a friend why the United States set up a national banking system. Read each sentence below. Decide which sentences are relevant to what you will say. Put a check in front of the relevant sentences.

_____ 1. Many different kinds of money were in use in the early United States.

_____ 2. There was no one medium of exchange in the United States.

_____ 3. Some people felt banks had too much power.

_____ 4. The United States did not have a stable money supply.

_____ 5. State banks do business under rules set up by state governments.

SAVING, BORROWING, and INVESTING

CHAPTER 10

Consider as you read

- How can people save money?
- How do people help the economy by saving money?
- Why do people choose to borrow money?

In a free enterprise system, no one can tell you what to do with your money. You can spend your money in any way you wish. Of course, every spending decision has an opportunity cost. When you spend on one thing, you give up others.

Many people choose not to spend all their money as soon as they get it. They choose to save part of what they make. There are good reasons to save.

Reasons for Saving

Things like houses and cars cost a lot of money. Most people cannot pay for a house or car all at once. One way to get the

Many people save money for large purchases.

money for a house or car is to save it. But it can take a very long time to save that much money. Most people save enough money to pay part of the cost, and then they borrow the rest.

Suppose you want a car that costs $10,000. You plan to borrow $8,000 from a bank and pay the rest in cash. The $2,000 cash you pay is called a **down payment**. Most places that lend money require a down payment before they lend money. One reason people save is to be able to make a down payment on a large purchase.

Another reason for saving is large bills that come due just once or twice a year. Each month people may save part of the money they will need. For example, the taxes on a house may be $600 a year. This money must be paid all at once. By saving $50 each month, the money will be there when it is needed.

There is a saying called Murphy's Law that goes like this: If something can go wrong, it will. And often, when things go wrong, they do so when you can least afford it. Your car breaks down three days before payday. You have no money to get it fixed. And you have no way to get to work. Or you get sick and can't work for a week. There is not enough money to buy food and pay the rent.

Most people have car trouble or sickness once in a while. They know that sooner or later, something will go wrong. To make these times easier to get through, they save some money to pay such bills.

down payment
the cash you pay out of your pocket when you borrow money

Every year people must pay taxes.

One reason for saving money is to buy some expensive good.

Many people save to pay bills they know they will have many years from now. People save to send a child to college. They put money away while they are young so that when they are old, they can live without working.

Finally, some people save just so they will have money. Perhaps they have more than they need to live. They take the rest and put it aside. They may wish to leave the money to their children. Or they may wish to leave money to help fight disease or other problems.

People save money for many reasons. In a free enterprise system, we are all free to make these choices.

Ways To Save

There are many ways to save. One way is just to hide the money until it is needed. However, this is not a good way to save. The money may be lost or stolen. The money also does not earn interest. You could put the money in your checking account. But often you will spend the money.

Most people find it easiest to save if they have a savings account. Savings accounts are different from checking accounts. Savings accounts earn interest. Each month the bank pays you for leaving your money there. The amount of interest is usually about five percent. This means that each year the bank will pay you $5 for every $100 in your savings account.

Some kinds of savings accounts let you write checks. Banks pay more interest on these accounts. But there is a catch. You may have to keep a certain amount of money in the account to earn the higher interest. And you may be able to write only a few checks a month on the account.

Another kind of savings account is the **time deposit**. Time deposits pay more interest than other savings accounts but only if you leave the money in the bank for the full time.

People who work for themselves often have **retirement accounts**. You can take money from a retirement account only when you are between the ages of 59 and 72. If you take the money out sooner, you must pay tax on it.

Another way to put money aside for the future is to buy stock. Stock is part ownership in a company. When the company makes a profit, it pays each person who owns stock. People who buy stock are **investing**. People who buy stock hope its price will go up. Then they can sell the stock and make a profit. Some people invest in land. If the price goes up, they can sell and make a profit. Other people invest by buying things a company needs to make more goods. Investing is an important way people put money aside.

Investing is a risk. When you invest money, there is a chance you will not get it back. The price of stock or land may fall. A business may fail. Most people invest money only after they

time deposit
money you agree to leave with the bank for a certain number of months or years

retirement accounts
special kinds of savings accounts

investing
buying something in the hope of making a profit by selling it later

A man meets with a woman who will help him to invest his money.

have saved enough to see them through hard times. They invest only the money they can afford to lose.

Buying on Credit

Even if you save, sometimes you may borrow money to buy things. This is called buying on **credit**. People use credit for two main reasons. First, credit lets people get what they want without waiting. If you buy a car on credit, you can drive it while you pay for it. If you saved to buy the car, you would have to wait until you had all the money before you could get the car. A second reason people buy on credit is to spread payments out over time. It may take twenty or thirty years to pay for a house. Most people could not buy a house without credit.

There are many kinds of credit. Credit cards let you buy goods now and pay for them later. A loan from a bank to buy a house or car is credit. Charge accounts are credit. Every time you use credit, you are borrowing money. This money must be paid back. You must also pay interest for the use of the money you borrowed.

The cost of credit is important. Knowing the cost of credit can help you make decisions about using credit. For example, if you borrow $500 to buy a television set, the set will cost more than $500. At twelve percent interest for one year, the set will cost about $530. Each month you will have to pay about $45. Before buying on credit, you must decide if you can afford the monthly payments and the extra cost of using credit.

Any store or bank that lends money must tell people what the cost of credit is. It is your right to know the cost of credit. Before you buy on credit, ask to know three things. How much will the interest be? How long will the payments go on? What will be the total amount to be paid? Knowing these three things can help you decide if you should use credit.

How Saving, Borrowing, and Investing Affect the Economy

Saving, borrowing, and investing are very important to the economy. They help keep businesses in the United States going. They help keep workers on the job.

credit
the buying of goods with borrowed money

Credit Cards Accepted

Saving and borrowing work together. When someone puts money into savings, the money does not just sit in the bank. The money one person saves, another person borrows. The person who borrows money spends it.

Sometimes the borrower is a business. For example, a company may be able to make 500 gallons of ice cream a day. But it has only one truck to deliver the ice cream. The truck can deliver only 250 gallons a day. With two trucks, the company could sell twice as much. The people who own the company decide to borrow money to buy a new truck. They are investing in the company. They hope to make more money. With the extra money, they can hire more workers to make even more ice cream. These workers will then have money to spend and save.

The money each of us saves or spends helps many other people. Money other people save or spend helps us. When we save money, we make it possible for someone else to borrow. When we invest in a business, we help that business grow. These things work together to help keep our economy strong.

Many people save money for when they retire.

Comprehension — *Write a Paragraph*

Use six or more words or phrases in the box to write a paragraph that tells how saving, borrowing, and investing help the economy.

saving	borrowing	investing	hire	businesses
workers	grow	economy	spend	strong

_____

_____

_____

_____

_____

_____

_____

_____

Vocabulary — *Exclusions*

One word or phrase in each group does not belong. Find the word and cross it out. Then write a sentence that tells how the other words are alike.

1. down payment
   large bills
   college tuition
   savings account

   _____

   _____

   _____

2. time deposit
   credit
   buying stock
   savings account

   _____

   _____

   _____

3. land
   stock
   things a company needs
   payments

   _____

   _____

   _____

4. buy now and pay later
   spread payments out
   investing
   pay interest

   _____

   _____

   _____

Critical Thinking — *Fact and Opinion*

Read each sentence below. If the sentence is a fact, write **F** on the blank. If the sentence is an opinion, write **O** on the blank. If the sentence gives both a fact and an opinion, write **FO** on the blank, and circle the part of the sentence that is an opinion.

_____ 1. Most places that lend money require a down payment before they lend the money.

_____ 2. Saving can help you pay unexpected bills, and everyone should save for this reason.

_____ 3. Most people find it easiest to save if they have a savings account, because most people are not good at saving.

_____ 4. Time deposits pay more interest than other savings accounts.

_____ 5. People who work for themselves should have a retirement account.

_____ 6. Knowing the cost of credit can help you decide whether you should borrow.

_____ 7. Saving, borrowing, and investing help keep our economy strong.

_____ 8. Each person should save at least one dollar in every ten earned.

_____ 9. There are many reasons to save money, but saving for a down payment is the most important.

_____ 10. Some savings accounts allow you to write checks.

Reading a Table

The table below shows three loan plans for two loan amounts. Study the table. Then answer the questions.

Monthly Loan Payments

Amount of Loan	Interest Rate	1-year Loan			2-year Loan			3-year Loan		
		Interest to be Paid	Monthly Payment	Total to Repay	Interest to be Paid	Monthly Payment	Total to Repay	Interest to be Paid	Monthly Payment	Total to Repay
$1,000	10%	$100	$ 91	$1,100	$200	$ 50	$1,200	$ 300	$ 36	$1,300
	12%	$120	$ 93	$1,120	$240	$ 51	$1,240	$ 360	$ 37	$1,360
	18%	$180	$ 98	$1,180	$360	$ 56	$1,360	$ 540	$ 42	$1,540
$2,500	10%	$250	$229	$2,750	$500	$125	$3,000	$ 750	$ 90	$3,250
	12%	$300	$233	$2,800	$600	$129	$3,100	$ 900	$ 94	$3,400
	18%	$450	$245	$2,950	$900	$141	$3,400	$1,350	$106	$3,850

Note: Interest and monthly payments were calculated using simple interest. Actual payments and interest would be less on installment loans.

1. What two loan amounts are shown in the table? _____

2. What interest rates are shown in the table? _____

3. What lengths of loan are shown in the table? _____

4. How much interest would be paid on a $1,000 loan at 12% interest for two years?

_____

5. What would be the monthly payment on a $2,500 loan at 18% interest for three years?

_____

6. If you borrowed $2,500 at 18% interest for three years, how much would you

actually pay back? _____

7. How much could you save by paying back a $2,500 loan at 18% interest in one year

instead of three? _____

8. How much could you save on a three-year loan by borrowing $2,500 at a bank that charges 12% interest instead of using a credit card that charges 18% interest?

_____

The FEDERAL RESERVE SYSTEM

◆

CHAPTER 11

Consider as you read

- How is money controlled in the United States?
- What happens to checks that have been used to buy something?

◆

Most people keep their money in banks. They do this because banks keep money safe. Banks make it easy to pay bills far away. Banks loan money. All these things take a lot of work and worry out of handling money.

Our country has a bank, too. The Federal Reserve System is the bank of the United States. The Federal Reserve System is often called the Fed for short. The Fed is a very important part of our economic system.

How the Federal Reserve System Is Set Up

The Fed is made up of about six thousand banks all across the United States. If a bank has the word "national" in its name, it is a member of the Fed.

This is the main bank of the Federal Reserve System.

The board of governors runs the Fed.

The Fed is run by seven people called the board of governors. These people are appointed by the president. They decide how the Fed should be run.

The Fed is divided into twelve parts, or districts. Each district has a Federal Reserve Bank. Each district bank serves its part of the country. The main office of the Fed is in Washington, D.C.

Even though the Fed was set up by the government, the government does not own it. The Fed is owned by its six thousand member banks.

What the Federal Reserve System Does

The Fed makes sure that member banks do business according to certain rules. And it provides a number of services to member banks.

Clearing checks is one service of the Fed. When someone writes a check, there has to be a way for that check to be sent to the bank so the money can be paid. The Fed provides that way. This is called check clearing. It works this way. Suppose you live in Buffalo, New York. You order a shirt from a company in Los Angeles and send it a check. First, the company takes the check to its bank in Los Angeles. The bank then sends the check to its Federal Reserve Bank in San Francisco. This district bank then sends the check to the district Federal Reserve Bank in New York. The check is then sent to your bank in Buffalo. The amount of the check is subtracted from your account. Then word is sent to the bank in Los Angeles to put the money in the company's account.

You can see that clearing checks is a very important service of the Fed. This service makes it easy to send money anywhere in the United States.

The Fed also lends money to member banks. Yes, even banks need to borrow money sometimes. Banks do not keep all their money on hand at all times. Most of it has been lent. Sometimes banks need extra cash. Often this happens on paydays when many people cash checks. Banks borrow money from the Fed to have enough cash on hand on these days.

How banks do business is very important. For example, banks must be careful about loaning money. They must be sure that people can pay the money back. Otherwise, the bank could run out of money. It would then have to go out of business.

If a bank does run out of money, what happens to the people who had money in the bank? What if you put your

Sometimes banks need extra money, such as on paydays.

Banks advertise their interest rates.

paycheck in the bank on Friday, and it went out of business on Monday? If it does, you may not lose your money. The Federal Deposit Insurance Corporation (FDIC) was set up to pay people their money when banks fail. Every bank that is a member of the Fed must also be a member of the FDIC. Other banks can join, too. Almost all banks are members of the FDIC. The Fed and the FDIC work together to see that banks are careful about loaning money. This cuts down on the number of banks that fail and go out of business.

Controlling the Money Supply

The main job of the Fed is to control the supply of money in the United States. The supply of money includes all the **currency** and all the amount of money in checking accounts. The Fed has several ways of controlling the money supply.

You will recall that banks loan out the money people put in savings accounts. However, banks cannot loan out all the money people save. Banks must keep back part of the money. This helps make sure they will have cash to pay people who want money from their account.

The Fed tells banks how much money they must keep back. The amount of money each bank must keep back is called the reserve requirement. The **reserve requirement** can be as much as 22 percent of the money people have put in the bank.

currency
bills and coins

reserve requirement
the amount of money a bank holds back

The Fed uses the reserve requirement to control how much money banks can lend. If the Fed tells banks to keep more money in reserve, they have less to loan. This cuts back on the supply of money. If the Fed lowers the reserve requirement, banks have more money to lend. This makes the money supply bigger.

When the Fed loans money to member banks, it charges them interest. The amount of interest the Fed charges member banks is called the discount rate. The Fed uses the discount rate to help control the money supply. Here is how it works. Let's say a bank borrows money from the Fed. It then loans the money to its customers. The bank charges customers a higher rate of interest than it pays the Fed. This is how the bank makes a profit.

If the Fed raises the discount rate, banks must pay more to borrow money. So they borrow less. This means they have less to lend. The money supply gets smaller. If the Fed lowers the discount rate, banks pay less to borrow. This encourages them to borrow more and lend more. The money supply gets larger.

This bank was closed by the Fed because it had loaned money that was not being paid back.

When the Fed uses tight money, businesses may not hire as many workers.

"Easy" and "Tight" Money

If there is a large supply of money, banks have plenty of money to lend. Loans are easy to get. Interest rates are low. People will borrow money to buy cars, homes, and other things. The total amount of spending in the economy goes up.

When the Fed wants to encourage people to spend more, it increases the money supply. This is called **easy money**. Easy money is used to make the economy grow. Businesses will borrow money to buy new machines. They may hire new workers.

easy money
a large supply of money

Sometimes the economy grows too fast. People have too much money to spend. Businesses cannot produce enough goods to keep up with demand. Prices go up. Then the Fed may cut back on the money supply. This is called **tight money**. Tight money is used to slow the economy down. Businesses may cut back production. Some workers may lose their jobs.

tight money
a small supply of money

Controlling the money supply is a big job. It is also very hard to do. However, it is very important. Controlling the money supply helps keep the economy from slowing down too much or from growing too quickly.

Comprehension – *Write the Questions*

Below are the answers for some questions from this chapter. Read each answer. Then write your own questions above each answer. Use the question words to help you.

1. What _____ ?

   This is another name for the Federal Reserve System.

2. Who _____ ?

   These people run the Federal Reserve System.

3. What _____ ?

   This makes it possible to pay bills by check anywhere in the United States.

4. What _____ ?

   This pays people back if their money is lost when a bank fails.

5. What _____ ?

   This is the part of the money people put in banks that cannot be loaned out.

6. What _____ ?

   This is interest charged by the Fed on money loaned to member banks.

Vocabulary – *Find the Meaning*

Write the word or phrase that best completes each sentence on the blank.

1. The **Federal Reserve System** is the _____ of the United States.

   district   FDIC   bank

2. The **discount rate** is the _____ that the Fed charges member banks.

   amount of interest   reserve requirement   money supply

3. The **FDIC** makes sure that when banks _____ , people get their money back.

   open   lend   fail

4. Checks and **currency** are _____ that people put in the bank.

savings   money   reserve

5. A decrease in the money supply, called **tight money**, means it may

be _____ to borrow money.

easy   difficult   good

6. **Easy money** means that the Fed wants the money supply

to be _____ .

small   large   the same

7. The Fed uses the **reserve requirement** to control how much money banks

can _____ .

borrow   lend   spend

Critical Thinking — *Cause and Effect*

Choose a cause or an effect from **Group B** to complete each sentence in **Group A**. Write the letter of the correct answer on the blank.

Group A

1. Our government wanted the money we put in banks to be safe,

so _____ .

2. _____ , so it tells banks how much money to keep back and not loan out.

3. When the economy slows down too much, the Fed wants to speed it up,

so _____ .

4. When a bank takes a check, it wants

to collect the money, so _____ .

5. _____ , so the Fed uses tight money to slow the economy down.

Group B

a. It lowers the discount rate.

b. It set up the Federal Deposit Insurance Corporation.

c. It sends the check to be cleared through the Federal Reserve System.

d. The Fed wants to be sure banks have enough cash on hand.

e. The money supply is too large, and prices rise too fast.

Money in History

What do you think of when you think of money? You probably see dollar bills, quarters, dimes, pennies. These things are the money we know. However, many other things have been used for money. Long ago in Africa, people used beads and shells, cloth, tools made of iron, and salt. The people who lived on the Yap Islands used large, round stones with a hole in the middle. Some of these stones were eight feet across and very heavy. They may have been the largest money ever used.

Many things used for money seem strange to us today. Long ago in China, tea leaves were pressed into bricks and used for money. The same was done with cheese long ago in Russia. Some Native Americans made wampum. Wampum was beads made of clam shells. White beads were worth half as much as black beads. Wampum was legally used as money by both colonists and Native Americans. When some colonists found they could dye the white beads black and double their value, people stopped using wampum.

Money was actually invented very early in human history. Coins were first made by the Chinese, perhaps as early as several thousand years ago. The best-known early coins were made in Lydia about 700 B.C. Lydia was a country in what is now western Turkey. People in India were also making coins at about the same time.

You might think that paper money came next. Actually, checks were invented before paper money. Checks written on clay tablets were used in Assyria, part of the Middle East, a hundred years before coins were made in Lydia.

Paper money was first used in China, perhaps as early as 300 B.C. It was not until the 1500s that people in Europe began using paper money.

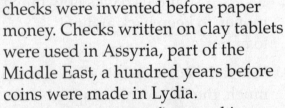

Coins were used over two thousand years ago in Europe.

Early money did not look like our money of today. The first Chinese "coins" were actually tiny shovels, hoes, knives, and other tools made of bronze or copper. The coins made in Lydia looked more like our coins. They were small, flat, round pieces of metal. The value of the coin was stamped into it.

Look at a dime, quarter, or half-dollar. Have you ever wondered why these coins have ridges around the edges? Once coins were made of gold or silver. People would shave bits of metal off the edges of the coins. These tiny bits would then be sold. However, the coins got smaller and smaller! Finally a five-dollar coin might be worth only half as much. To stop people from shaving the coins, ridges were put around the edges. Anyone who saw a coin without ridges would know it was not worth as much. They could refuse to take it.

Write About It

On a separate sheet of paper, write a paragraph that tells the advantages and disadvantages of some of the different kinds of money you have read about.

People in Italy during the 1400s saved their money at a bank like this one.

UNIT 5

GOVERNMENT and the ECONOMY

YOUR TAX DOLLARS AT WORK

In recent years the size of government has greatly increased. About seventeen million people work for state and national governments — more than for any other employer. Five times as many people work for state and local governments today as did fifty years ago. The number of people working for the national government has stayed about the same.

Even greater growth has taken place in government spending. State and local governments today spend about sixty times as much as they did fifty years ago. The national government spends about twelve times as much.

The government has many jobs. Not only does it protect the people of the nation, but it provides many services. It builds and repairs highways. The mail is delivered by government workers. The rights of consumers are protected by the government. It makes sure that the meat and vegetables we eat are safe.

In order to pay for the many services it provides, government collects money from the people. We pay taxes. This tax money covers the costs of protection and the many other jobs of the government.

Today government is our country's biggest business. What it does has a great impact on our economy. To put it another way, when the government sneezes, we all catch cold.

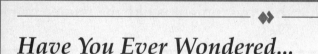

Have You Ever Wondered...

- Why do we have taxes?

- How does the government spend your tax money?

- Why do governments often spend more money than they take in?

These questions and others will be answered in this unit. You will learn how the government controls the economy. You will read about ways consumers are protected by the government. You will learn why government and not private business provides things such as police and fire protection and parks. You will learn how government uses tax money and spending policies to try to keep the whole economy growing.

GOVERNMENT and the ECONOMY

CHAPTER 12

Consider as you read

- Why is the government part of free enterprise?

- How does the government make sure the economy runs smoothly?

Every day the news is filled with stories about government and the economy. The president may talk about the need for more jobs. Congress may pass a new law that tells business owners what to do. The courts may rule that a television ad gives people the wrong idea about a product.

If the United States has a free enterprise system, why does the government have so much to do with the economy? The answer is that the government is like the referee in a football

Government can affect the economy in many ways. Providing highways for people to travel to work is one.

The railroad system in the United States was a monopoly. After the Sherman Antitrust Act railroad monopolies were not legal.

game. The players are all the businesses and consumers. The referee sees that everyone follows the rules. That way, everyone has an equal chance to win.

The government acts in several ways to help the economy. It sets some rules that businesses must follow. It protects consumers' rights. It provides some goods and services itself. It works to help people who cannot provide for themselves.

Government Regulation of the Economy

By setting rules businesses must follow, the government promotes fair competition. The first very large businesses in the United States grew up in the late 1800s and early 1900s. Railroads became very big business. So did steel making. Some railroads and steel companies grew very large. They became so big they could control prices. They were monopolies. In a monopoly there is no competition. There is no other place for people to go. Without competition, a business can charge whatever it wants. This is good for the business. However, it can be very bad for everyone else.

In 1890, the United States passed an important law. The Sherman Antitrust Act made monopolies against the law. It said that no business could limit competition. This law is still in use today.

The government promotes fair competition in other ways. One way is by setting rules for how businesses treat their workers. Workers must be paid at least a minimum wage. The work place must be made safe. Without these rules, a business could pay low wages and not spend money to protect workers. The costs for the business would be lower. Then it could sell its products cheaper than companies that treated their workers well. Government rules keep businesses from treating their workers poorly.

Some laws make businesses clean up pollution. These laws promote fair competition, too. A company that does not spend money to clean up pollution has lower costs than companies that do. The company that does not clean up can sell its products cheaper. Laws against pollution help keep this from happening. These laws protect people's health as well as land, air, and water.

Protection of Consumers

Consumers buy the goods and services that businesses produce. In most cases, consumers do not know the people who run those businesses. Few of us know the people who boxed the cereal we ate for breakfast. We must depend on

Government sets rules to keep businesses from causing too much pollution.

Federal Laws Protecting Consumers

Date	Act	Purpose
1890	Sherman Antitrust Act	Prevented businesses from limiting competition
1906	Pure Food and Drug Act	Set standards for processing food and drugs
1938	Fair Labor Standards Act	Provided for a minimum wage, 40-hour work week, control of child labor
1960	Hazardous Substances Labeling Act	Required warning labels on dangerous household chemicals
1960	Child Protection Act	Stopped sale of dangerous toys
1966	Fair Packaging and Labeling Act	Required accurate labeling of goods
1967	Flammable Fabrics Act	Set safety standards for clothing
1968	Consumer Credit Protection Act	Required clear statement of interest and other loan costs

those people to give us clean, safe food. Laws see to it that this is the case.

Laws protect people who take drugs for their health. Firms that make drugs must test the drugs to be sure they are safe. Like food, all drugs must be made in clean places. Labels must tell exactly what is in the drugs. Consumers must be warned about bad things that can happen to people taking the drugs.

Many laws promote fair competition and protect consumers. Some of these laws are listed in the chart on this page.

Many government offices protect consumers. The Food and Drug Administration protects people from unsafe food and drugs. The Consumer Product Safety Commission sets rules that make toys and other products safe. You read about the Federal Deposit Insurance Corporation in Chapter 11. The FDIC makes sure that the money we put in banks is safe.

The Securities and Exchange Commission protects people who buy stock in companies. Companies that want to sell stock must work with the SEC. The companies must tell the SEC the truth about themselves. If the company is about to go out of business, the SEC can stop the sale of its stock.

Some people try to make money on the sale of stocks by using secrets. For example, someone may learn that a company is about to bring out a new product that everyone will want. The company will make plenty of money. Many people will want to buy its stock. The price of the stock will go up. The person who knows this secret can buy a lot of stock. After the price goes up, the stock can be sold. The person will make a lot of money. This is against the law. It is not fair to everyone else. The SEC works to stop this.

Public Goods

Some goods and services cannot be provided by private business. Think about roads. What would it be like if private business built all roads? If you had a house that needed a road, you would have to find someone to build that road for you. You might have to pay other people to let the road cross their land. Most people could not afford to pay for roads.

We have an army, navy, and air force to keep our country safe. What if each of us had to have our own army to protect us? Most of us could not afford an army. And it would be very easy for a country with a big army to defeat the many small armies in a war. This would place us all in danger.

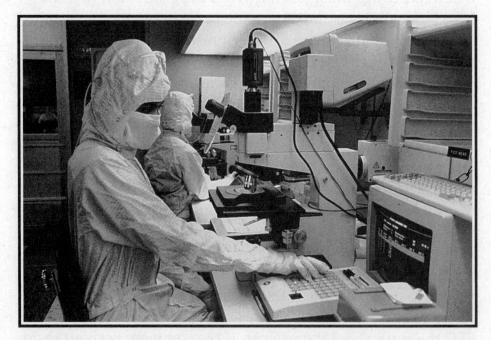

Learning the secrets about new products and using the knowledge to buy or sell stocks is not legal.

Providing protection through the military is a public good.

Things like roads and armies are called **public goods**. Education, parks, and police protection are also public goods. We all need the chance to go to school. We need parks to play in. We need protection from crime. It would be very hard for businesses to provide these things.

Public goods are often very costly. But they are things that everyone needs and should have. Government is all of us working together. We use government to provide the goods and services that private businesses cannot.

public goods
goods or services that the government provides for everyone

Promoting Economic Well-Being

One job of the government is to promote the **general welfare**. This job is so important that it is one of six listed in the Constitution.

Many things make up the economic health of the nation. We need strong businesses. We need a strong banking system. We need fair competition among businesses. Most of all, however, we need strong, healthy people who can do their part to make the country strong.

Our free enterprise system is based on competition. But some people cannot compete as well as others. Some people become too sick or too old to work. Some people do not get enough education to get a good job. Other people lose their jobs and have trouble finding another. All these people need help. With help, they may be able to solve their problems.

general welfare
the economic health of the nation

125

They can once again do their part to produce goods and services.

The government sends money to people who can show they need help. Sometimes the money is for medical bills. Sometimes it is for better housing or training for a job. Some people get money to help them buy food. Old people are one of the largest groups to receive help. People who are out of work can also receive help. The government sends them money while they look for a new job.

All these payments help the whole country, not just the people who receive them. People spend the money they receive. This money goes to businesses and helps them pay their workers. The government payments help keep the demand for goods and services high. This helps keep the economy strong.

The government helps people who are unemployed find work.

Comprehension – *Reviewing Important Facts*

Match the sentence in **Group A** with the word or phrase from **Group B** that the sentence explains. Write the letter of the correct answer on the blank.

Group A

_____ 1. This said that monopolies were against the law.

_____ 2. In order for this to happen, the government in the United States sets rules for businesses.

_____ 3. This government office protects people from unsafe food and drugs.

_____ 4. This government office helps see that toys are safe.

_____ 5. This government office protects people who buy stock in companies.

_____ 6. This government office helps make sure the money you put in banks is safe.

_____ 7. Education, police, and fire protection are all examples of this government service.

_____ 8. The government promotes this to help keep the economy strong.

Group B

a. Federal Deposit Insurance Corporation

b. Food and Drug Administration

c. general welfare

d. Sherman Antitrust Act

e. Consumer Product Safety Commission

f. public goods

g. fair competition

h. Securities and Exchange Commission

Vocabulary — *Write a Paragraph*

Use six or more words or phrases in the box to write a paragraph that tells how the government works to help the economy.

rules	referee	fair competition	protect
consumers	safe	private business	public goods
economic health	education	payments	

_____

_____

_____

_____

_____

_____

Critical Thinking — *Distinguishing Relevant Information*

Imagine that you have to tell a friend how the government promotes the general welfare. Read each sentence below. Decide which sentences are relevant to what you will say. Put a check in front of the relevant sentences.

_____ 1. We need strong businesses and a safe banking system.

_____ 2. We need fair competition among businesses.

_____ 3. Railroads became very large businesses in the late 1800s.

_____ 4. The government sends money to people who need help.

_____ 5. Government provides some goods and services that private businesses cannot.

_____ 6. Some people try to make money on the sale of stocks by using secret information.

_____ 7. Some people and businesses cannot compete as well as others.

GOVERNMENT PAYS ITS BILLS

CHAPTER 13

Consider as you read

- How does the government pay for the goods and services it provides?

- How does government spending affect the nation's economy?

taxes
money we pay to the government to cover the cost of public goods

sales taxes
taxes on the sale of goods and services

property taxes
taxes on the value of property

Taxes are a very necessary part of our economic system. Since we expect many services from our government, we must pay the cost of these services. There are many kinds of taxes. Here we will look at taxes that are paid to one of three levels of government. These levels are local, state, and national.

Local Taxes

Local taxes are paid to cities, counties, and schools. Local governments receive most of their money from two kinds of taxes — **sales taxes** and **property taxes**.

The government collects taxes to provide services like safe highways.

NOTICE !

Gasoline Prices Include:

29 Cents Federal Tax per gallon

7 % State Tax per gallon

People have a right to know what taxes they are paying.

If you buy a new car, you may pay a sales tax. This tax will be based on the price of the car. The higher the price of the car, the higher the tax will be. You may pay sales taxes on meals or clothes you buy. Sales taxes are also placed on services. In fact, sales taxes are probably placed on more different kinds of things than any other kind of tax.

People who own land or buildings pay property taxes. The property tax is used by almost all local governments. In fact, about eight out of every ten dollars collected in taxes by local governments come from property taxes. Property taxes pay for most of our police and fire protection. They pay for our schools and our parks.

People who own property may pay taxes to a city or a county government. They may also pay taxes to a school district. Each of these provides different services. But they all tax the same piece of property to pay for those services. Property taxes can be very expensive.

State Taxes

Most states also use sales and property taxes. Often they tax the same goods and services as local governments. Take the sales tax, for example. When you buy a soda, you probably pay a sales tax. The store keeper collects the tax from you. Part of the money is sent to the state. Part is sent to the local government.

Some states also have an **income tax**. If a person **earns** a lot of money, his or her income taxes are high. States use income taxes to pay for goods and services in the same way that sales and property taxes are used.

National Taxes

Most of the national government's money comes from just three taxes. One is the income tax on money people earn. There is also an income tax on the money businesses earn. Finally, there is a social security tax. Income taxes may be spent for any government services. Social security taxes are spent to help people who are too old or too sick to work.

About half of all the national government's money comes from the income tax. This money is held out of people's pay each time they are paid. The same is true of the social security tax. Income taxes on people and businesses plus social security taxes make up about eight out of every ten dollars the national government collects.

Taxes take about 29 cents out of every dollar earned in the United States. Many people feel this is too high. However,

Part of our taxes are spent to help people in need. Here government workers are helping people who don't earn enough money.

The government pays for firefighters to keep us safe.

Americans pay lower taxes than people in many countries. In Sweden, for example, people pay almost 51 cents of every dollar in taxes. The more services we get from our government, the more we must pay in taxes.

How Governments Spend Our Money

Local, state, and national governments spend huge sums of money. Where does all the money go? State and local governments spend most of their money on schools. They also spend much money on highways, police and fire protection, and aid to the poor.

The national government spends about 48 out of every 100 dollars on benefits such as social security. The second largest amount of money — 18 dollars out of 100 — is spent on armed forces and security. These numbers change from time to time. When the number of older people increases, there is more money spent on benefits. More money is spent on the armed forces during wars.

It may surprise you to learn what the national government spends the third-largest amount of money on. About 14 of every 100 dollars is spent on interest. This interest is on the **national debt**.

People often spend more money than they make. Governments sometimes do, too. This is called **deficit spending**. People and governments make up the difference between what they spend and what they earn in the same way. They borrow.

national debt
money the national government owes

deficit spending
spending more than you earn

132

The national government is a very large borrower. There is no bank with enough money to lend the government all the money it needs to borrow. The government borrows money from many places. If you own a United States Savings Bond, you have loaned the government money. There are several kinds of government bonds. People, banks, businesses, cities, states, and even other countries buy these bonds. About twelve out of every one hundred dollars is owed to people in other countries.

Spending, Taxes, Debt, and the Economy

Government spending affects the whole economy. Think of government as a very large consumer. Its spending sends messages to producers about what to produce. For example, the air force may order thousands of new planes. This helps the economy grow. Businesses make more money. More people have jobs. The government collects more in taxes. On the other hand, cuts in government spending slow the economy down.

Taxes are also used to make the economy either grow or slow down. Suppose people have plenty of money to spend. They buy lots of goods. Prices start to go up. Government can

The government sells United States Savings Bonds to pay for the services it provides.

133

Many Americans spend time in public parks, which are paid for by the government with our taxes.

fight this by raising taxes. People have less money to spend after they pay taxes. So they buy less. Demand falls, and prices stay low.

The opposite can also happen. Sometimes people may not have enough money. They can't buy enough goods to keep businesses going. Prices fall so low that businesses cannot make a profit. Government can cut taxes. People will then have more money to spend. They will buy more. Prices will rise.

Government borrowing affects the economy. When the government borrows a lot of money, it creates a high demand for money. The high demand makes interest rates go up. This makes it harder for other people to borrow money.

Some people feel the government should spend enough to keep the economy strong. Other people feel the government needs to cut the national debt. Most people do not want to raise taxes or cut the services they receive from the government. For the last thirty years, the government has followed a **fiscal policy** of deficit spending. It is likely that people will continue to disagree over fiscal policy for many years to come.

fiscal policy
the way the government uses taxing, spending, and borrowing to affect the economy

Vocabulary — *Match Up*

Choose a word or phrase from the box to complete each sentence. Write that word or phrase on the blank.

income tax	fiscal policy	sales tax	taxes
national debt	property taxes	deficit spending	

1. We pay _____ to the government to cover the cost of public goods.

2. A tax based on the price you pay for something is a _____ .

3. _____ are based on the value of property.

4. The tax you pay on the money you earn is an _____ .

5. The money our government owes is the _____ .

6. If you spend more than you make, this is called _____ .

7. How the government decides to tax, spend, and borrow is

   its _____ .

Comprehension — *Write the Answer*

Write one or more sentences to answer each question.

1. Where do cities, counties, and states get most of their money? _____

   _____

2. What is the difference between a sales tax and a property tax?

   _____

3. What is the biggest single source of income for the national government?

   _____

4. What are social security taxes used for? _____

   _____

5. About how many cents out of each dollar earned do Americans pay in taxes?

   _____

6. What do governments use tax money for? _____

   _____

7. If the government spends more money than it takes in, how does it make up

   the difference? _____

   _____

8. How can the government use taxes to make the economy grow? _____

   _____

Critical Thinking — *Drawing Conclusions*

Read the paragraph below and the sentences that follow it. Put a check in front of the conclusions that can be drawn from the paragraph.

> Our local, state, and national governments provide many services. Some of these services are things we cannot do for ourselves. Other services are things it would be hard for private business to do. Governments use tax money to pay for these services. Sometimes borrowed money is used as well. Government is a very large consumer of goods and services.

_____ 1. People work together through government to provide public goods.

_____ 2. Goods and services provided by governments are not free.

_____ 3. Taxes in the United States are too high.

_____ 4. Sometimes governments spend more money than they make in taxes.

_____ 5. Government is both a producer and a consumer.

_____ 6. Deficit spending is bad for the economy.

Using Energy Efficiency Ratings in Choosing Appliances

Use the energy label shown below to answer the questions that follow.

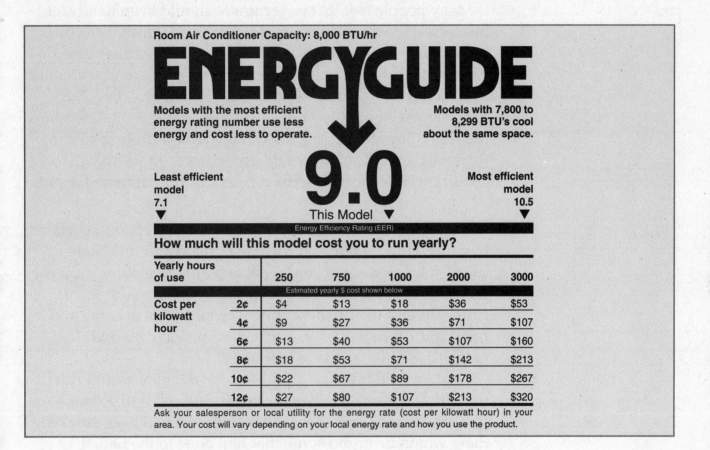

Room Air Conditioner Capacity: 8,000 BTU/hr

ENERGYGUIDE

Models with the most efficient energy rating number use less energy and cost less to operate.

Models with 7,800 to 8,299 BTU's cool about the same space.

9.0

Least efficient model
7.1 ▼

Most efficient model
10.5 ▼

This Model ▼

Energy Efficiency Rating (EER)

How much will this model cost you to run yearly?

Yearly hours of use		250	750	1000	2000	3000
		Estimated yearly $ cost shown below				
Cost per kilowatt hour	2¢	$4	$13	$18	$36	$53
	4¢	$9	$27	$36	$71	$107
	6¢	$13	$40	$53	$107	$160
	8¢	$18	$53	$71	$142	$213
	10¢	$22	$67	$89	$178	$267
	12¢	$27	$80	$107	$213	$320

Ask your salesperson or local utility for the energy rate (cost per kilowatt hour) in your area. Your cost will vary depending on your local energy rate and how you use the product.

1. What rating does this appliance have? _____

2. What are the ratings for the least and most efficient models like this one?

   _____

3. Suppose electricity in your area costs 6 cents per kilowatt hour, and you use an air conditioner about 1,000 hours per year. How much will this model cost you to run

   for a year? _____

4. At 8 cents per kilowatt hour, how much will this model cost to run for 3,000 hours

   per year? _____

Government on Patrol: The Jungle

Many people feel that government should keep hands off business. However, there are some cases in which everyone agrees government should step in. Most Americans agree that government should make sure our food, drugs, and water are safe. Before 1906, this was not the case. A book called *The Jungle* changed people's minds. The book told Americans how the meat they ate was prepared. First Americans got sick to their stomachs. Then they told government to see that conditions like those described below never happened again.

"Bubbly Creek"…is really a great open sewer a hundred or two feet wide.…Here and there the grease and filth have caked solid, and…chickens walk about on it, feeding.…Every now and then the surface would catch on fire and burn furiously, and the fire department would have to come and put it out. Once however, a stranger came and started to gather this filth…to make lard out of….

Meat…would often be found sour, and…they would rub it up with soda to take away the smell, and sell it to be eaten on free-lunch counters;…Also, after the hams had been smoked, there would be found some that had gone to the bad. Formerly these had been sold as "Number Three Grade," but later on some…person had hit upon a new device, and now they would extract the bone, about which the bad part generally lay, and insert in the hole a white-hot iron. After this invention there was no longer Number One, Two, and Three Grade — there was only Number One Grade….

There was never the least attention paid to what was cut up for sausage;…There would be meat that had tumbled out on the floor, in the dirt and sawdust, where the workers

Making Sausage, 1900s

had tramped and spit….There would be meat stored in great piles in rooms…and thousands of rats would race about on it….These rats were **nuisances**, and the packers would put poisoned bread out for them; they would die, and then rats, bread, and meat would go into the **hoppers** together. This is no fairy story and no joke; the meat would be shovelled into carts, and the man who did the shoveling would not trouble to lift out even a rat even when he saw one — there were things that went into the sausage in comparison with which a poisoned rat was a tidbit….There were some jobs that it only paid to do once in a long time, and among these was the cleaning out of the waste-barrels. Every spring…dirt and rust and old nails and stale water…would be taken up and dumped into the hoppers with fresh meat, and sent out to the public's breakfast….All of their sausage came out of the same bowl, but when they came to wrap it they would stamp some of it "special," and for this they would charge two cents more a pound.

nuisances
something that annoys

hoppers
large pots

Write About It

On a separate sheet of paper, write a paragraph that tells why we need laws to protect public health.

Upton Sinclair wrote about places like this, where meat was not kept clean.

MEASURING ECONOMIC PERFORMANCE

Economic growth is a major goal of the United States. When the economy is growing, more people have jobs. Businesses make more money. The government collects more taxes and is better able to provide the public goods and services people want.

For much of our history, government has kept its hands off the economy. Boom times when many people had money were followed by hard times when many people were out of work.

One of the worst times was the Great Depression. In 1929, the economy went into a very bad time. It lasted for many years. Thousands of people were out of work. Many companies went out of business. The price of goods and services was very high, and many people could barely afford even a loaf of bread. Hundreds of banks failed.

The Great Depression of the 1930s shocked Americans. They had never seen the economy get so bad. During the 1920s, many people made good livings. They could hardly believe that things could turn so bad so quickly.

Americans decided that such hard times must not come again to the United States. Since the 1930s, our national government has kept a close watch over the economy. It tries to see that economic growth remains steady.

Have You Ever Wondered...

- Why do the prices of most things seem to keep going up?
- What does an increase in the Consumer Price Index mean to you?
- Why, if economic growth is good, can't we just let the economy grow as fast as it can?
- Why doesn't everyone benefit equally from economic growth?

The answers to these and other questions will be found in this unit. You will read about the ups and downs of our economy. You will learn how inflation and recession can affect you. You will read about what causes our economy to grow, and how economic growth can be both good and bad. You will learn that some groups in America are still struggling to win their fair share of the American dream.

The BUSINESS CYCLE

CHAPTER 14

Consider as you read

- How does the economy change?
- How do we measure how well the economy is doing?

---

business cycle
the process of the economy going from strong to weak

The economy is a little like a roller coaster. It goes up and down. As it does, it takes us all with it. Sometimes the ride is fun. Life is good. Most people have jobs. There is plenty of money. At other times the roller coaster ride is bumpy. We all have to hang on tight. Many people lose their jobs. Money is hard to get. Life can be a little scary.

The ups and downs of the economy are called the **business cycle**. The business cycle happens again and again. Each time, it brings good times and bad times.

People would rather live during good times. Government, consumers, and businesses all do things that affect the

The business cycle is like a roller coaster, sometimes going up and other times going down.

142

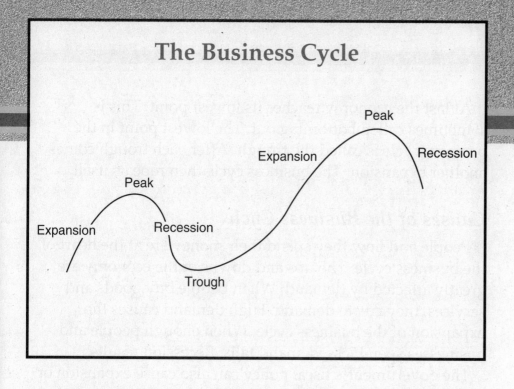

The Business Cycle

business cycle. Each works to make the good times last longer and the bad times go away more quickly.

Parts of the Business Cycle

The business cycle has four parts. Each cycle starts with a time when the economy grows. Businesses sell more and more goods. They may hire new workers. They may build new factories. This part of the business cycle is **expansion**. Expansion is a time of growth in the economy.

After a time of growth, the economy reaches a high point, like the highest place on a roller coaster ride. Unlike a roller coaster, the economy may stay at this high point for months or years. This is a time when almost everyone seems to have money. Jobs are easy to find. Businesses work hard to keep up with demand. Workers may be asked to work longer hours. This part of the business cycle is the **peak**. The peak is the part of the business cycle when business is at its best.

Just as with roller coasters, however, what goes up must come down. After the high point in the business cycle, the economy starts to slide lower. Sales of goods start to fall off. Business slows down. Some workers may lose their jobs. This part of the business cycle is a **recession**.

If a recession goes on for a very long time or if it is very bad, it is called a **depression**. During a depression, many businesses may fail. Many people lose their jobs. Most people have little money to spend.

expansion
growth

peak
high point

recession
a time when the economy has slowed down

depression
a time of very slow business activity

143

trough
the lowest point in business
activity

At last the economy reaches its lowest point. This is sometimes called bottoming out. The lowest point in the business cycle is called the **trough**. After each trough comes another expansion. The business cycle then repeats itself.

Causes of the Business Cycle

People and how they spend their money are at the heart of the business cycle. The ups and downs of the economy are greatly affected by demand. When people buy goods and services, they create demand. High demand causes the expansion of the business cycle. When enough people and businesses spend less, demand falls. Recession results.

The government's fiscal policy can also cause expansion or recession. If the government wants the economy to grow, it can cut taxes, spend more, or both. This policy helps create demand. The government may want the economy to slow down. Raising taxes and cutting spending takes money out of people's pockets. This policy causes demand to fall.

The Business Cycle at Work

We see signs of the business cycle at work in our lives every day. One of the signs we notice first is the price of the things we buy.

During the Great Depression, many people stood in long lines to get food.

144

When there is deflation many people are unemployed. They must stand in line to find work.

There are times when the prices of almost all goods and services go up. Such times often happen during the expansion and peak parts of the business cycle. It seems that every time you go to the store, prices are higher. The price of bread, meat, or gasoline may jump every month or every week. When the prices of almost everything are going up, we have **inflation**.

inflation
a time when prices of goods and services rise

Inflation can be a serious problem. If your pay does not go up as fast as prices of goods and services do, then you will not be able to buy as much. People who get the same amount of money each month are sometimes unable to buy all the things that they need. This often happens to retired people. They get only so much money a month. Inflation also hurts people who have saved money. As prices go up, their money will buy less.

Sometimes prices fall. Such times usually happen during the recession and trough parts of the business cycle. In **deflation**, most things cost less. However, wages may fall, too. Lower prices do not help people, since they have less money to spend. And during a recession, many people may lose their jobs.

deflation
a time when prices of goods and services drop

A person who wants work and cannot find a job is **unemployed**. When many people are out of work, demand for goods and services falls. People have less to spend. Business sales drop. Businesses cut back on production. They may need fewer workers. More people lose their jobs. Sometimes the number of unemployed people becomes very large.

unemployed
out of work

145

In the United States, we want every person who wants a job to have one. When people have jobs, they can do their part to keep the economy strong. They can buy goods and services. This takes care of their own wants and needs. The demand that they create makes jobs for other people. When most people are working, everyone is better off.

Keeping Track of Business Cycles

Inflation and recession hurt all of us. We try to keep them from happening. But how do we know inflation is starting? How do we know a recession is happening? The government gathers facts about these things. These facts tell us whether the economy is doing well or whether it is in trouble.

One fact the government gathers is the value of all new products made in the United States each year. This is called the **Gross National Product**, or GNP. If the GNP goes up, it means the economy is doing well. Factories are busy. People have jobs. However, if the GNP goes down for six months in a row, the business cycle is in recession.

The government also keeps track of prices. This helps us tell if inflation is starting. Each month the government checks the prices of four hundred things that people often buy. It

Gross National Product
the total value of all goods and services

When the economy is expanding, people spend more money.

When the economy is in expansion, then many businesses are able to hire new workers.

compares the prices paid with those paid at an earlier time. This price check is called the **Consumer Price Index**, or CPI. The Consumer Price Index is a comparison of prices today with prices in the past.

A small rise in the CPI is nothing to worry about. In a healthy, growing economy, the CPI will often rise three to five percent a year. A five percent rise means that an item that cost $1.00 a year ago now costs $1.05.

Larger rises in the CPI may signal trouble ahead. If the CPI rises ten percent or more a year, inflation could be a problem.

Keeping the economy growing without causing inflation is hard to do. This is one of the most important jobs our government has. You will read more about growth and the American economy in the next two chapters.

Consumer Price Index
a list showing the change in price of about four hundred goods

Comprehension — *Write a Paragraph*

Use six or more words or phrases in the box to write a paragraph that tells how the business cycle works.

demand	recession	spending	fiscal policy	peak	jobs
trough	economy	expansion	depression	grow	

_____

_____

_____

_____

_____

Vocabulary — *Find the Meaning*

Write the word or phrase that best completes each sentence on the blank.

1. The **expansion** part of the business cycle is a time of _____ .

    slow business   growth   recession

2. When the economy is in **recession**, it is _____ .

    speeding up   slowing down   staying the same

3. During the **peak** of the business cycle, workers will have _____ jobs than during a depression.

    more   fewer   as many

4. A very long, bad **recession** is a _____ .

    trough   depression   deflation

5. **Inflation** is a _____ in the price of almost everything.

    rise   fall   stable level

6. An **unemployed** person cannot find _____ .

enough work   a job   goods and services

7. The **Consumer Price Index** is a way of keeping track of _____ .

inflation only   deflation only   both inflation and deflation

Critical Thinking — *Categories*

Read the words in each group. Decide how they are alike. Write a title for each group on the blank beside each group. You may use the words in the box for all or part of each title.

fiscal policy	expansion	recession
business cycle	trough	Consumer Price Index

1. peak
   recession
   trough
   _____

2. growth
   new workers
   rising sales
   _____

3. business failures
   unemployed people
   bottoming out
   _____

4. easy or tight money
   government
   demand increases or falls
   _____

5. today's prices
   earlier prices
   inflation
   _____

6. falling sales
   slowing economy
   unemployed workers
   _____

ECONOMIC GROWTH

CHAPTER 15

---◆◆---

Consider as you read

- What causes the economy to grow?
- What are the good and bad effects of a growing economy?

---◆◆---

Sometimes we hear people talk about "the good old days." They often say things like, "Life was simpler then," "We ate a lot of beans," "Most of our clothes were homemade," "That old house was full of holes. It was air-conditioned in winter and heated in summer," "We didn't have all the things you young folks have today."

Why do we enjoy things today that our parents and grandparents did not have? The answer may surprise you. We have these things not because we are smarter than they were. We have them not because we have more money. We have more things today because of economic growth. When the Gross National Product (GNP) increases, there is economic growth. Economic growth allows us to have a better life.

Because of economic growth, people are better off today than they were twenty years ago.

Everyone shares in the Gross National Product.

How Economic Growth Helps Us

The GNP is like an apple pie we all help make. Each of us puts as many apples into the pie as we can. The more apples each of us puts in, the bigger the pie becomes. When it is time to eat the pie, we get a bigger slice from a big pie than we would get from a small pie. We all share in producing the GNP. If each of us produces more, the GNP grows. Each of us also helps consume the GNP. If the GNP is bigger, there is more for each of us to consume.

We live in a country with a large GNP. There are many goods and services for us to share. We call this a high **standard of living**. The more things there are for us to buy and enjoy, the higher the standard of living. Economic growth has given most of us a higher standard of living than our parents had. We have more goods and services that make our lives better. Our "piece of pie" is bigger than theirs was.

Economic growth does more than just give us a higher standard of living. Each year our country produces more goods and services. It takes added workers to keep up with the demand for more goods and services. Growth makes it possible for more people to have jobs.

More people working and paying taxes means that the government has more money. When the government has more

standard of living
the number of goods and services available to each person

151

money, it can do a better job of providing the public goods we need. Economic growth helps us have better schools. It helps us have better police and fire protection and better parks. The government can spend the added money on health programs and more highways. It can keep our army strong.

Sources of Economic Growth

Economic growth comes from three main sources. They are:
1. wise use of the factors of production,
2. use of inventions, and
3. increases in resources.

The factors of production are land, labor, and capital. To have economic growth, a country must use these factors well. For example, waste hurts economic growth. Once a resource has been used up, it is no longer there for us to use. Wise use of resources means getting the most we can out of them. Saving resources now will leave more to be used later. Wise use of our land and its resources means that we will have those things to use when we need them.

Labor must be used wisely, too. Workers must be educated. Businesses must give workers good tools to do their jobs. Workers must do their jobs quickly and well. If workers do

Educated workers are a source of economic growth.

The wise use of capital is a source of economic growth.

not have good tools, they may take too long to do a job. Or they may do it poorly, and it may have to be redone. Workers who do poor work or who waste time on the job hurt economic growth. Workers who do a good job in less time help economic growth. Making sure that workers do their jobs well helps economic growth.

Sometimes factories have more machines than they need. The machines run only part of the time. This is a waste of capital. Money was spent to buy the machines and put up buildings to hold them. Part of that money was wasted. It could have been spent on other things. A country that wastes too much of its capital has less money to spend on things it needs. Wise use of capital means that machines, tools, and buildings are kept busy as much of the time as possible.

Inventions often help economic growth. Inventions may help people do more work at a lower cost. A new plow may help farmers grow more food with less work. A new machine may turn out twice as much work as an old one. A new way to make something may save resources. All these things help economic growth by helping us make better use of land, labor, and capital.

Sometimes economic growth is caused by an increase in resources. Someone may find a new oil field. This increases our supply of oil. This oil can be used to make more goods and services. This helps economic growth.

An increase in the labor supply can also cause economic growth. Many factories began in the United States in the late 1800s. New workers were needed. Many people left farms to go to work in the new factories. Other people moved to the United States from other countries. All these people needed homes, food, and clothing. The demand for these things caused many businesses to grow. Without the workers, the factories could not have operated. With them, the factories were able to increase production. Our country enjoyed many years of economic growth.

Costs of Economic Growth

"You can't get something for nothing" is a common saying. In other words, nothing is free. There is a cost for everything we have. There are costs for economic growth, too. Many of these costs are hidden, but they are there. These costs include damage to the world we live in and to ourselves.

Look around you. You probably see many things that were made by people — chairs, tables, floors, walls, and books. Each of these things is made of wood, metal, or some other material. Each time we make something, we use up some of our natural resources. Some resources can be replaced. We can

Some resources, such as these redwoods, can be replaced.

Pollution is one cost of economic growth.

grow new trees to make more wood. Some resources cannot be replaced. We cannot make more oil. When we have used up all the world's oil, there will be no more.

The more economic growth we have, the faster we use up the earth's resources. This is a serious problem. Once all the earth's resources are gone, people will not be able to live here.

Pollution is another cost of economic growth. Pollution is the dirtying of our air, water, and soil. Many economic activities cause pollution. Farming throws dust into the air. Sprays used to kill insects put poisons into the water. Factories put things that can harm life into the air and water. Our cars put poisons into the air as we drive. The more economic growth we have, the more pollution we have. Someday all this pollution must be cleaned up. The cost of the cleanup will be very large. The money spent on cleaning up pollution cannot be used on other things.

Economic growth has also caused problems that are hard to put a price tag on. Many people have moved to cities to be near their jobs. Some cities have become very large. Sometimes there are more people than homes in a city. People must live where they are crowded together. When too many people are jammed together, there are problems. More people may get sick. There may be more crime. Schools may have too many children in each class. All this adds up to people who are not as happy as they could be.

Some groups of people in America have not shared equally in economic growth. They suffer more from the problems of economic growth than they gain from it. You will read about some of these people in the next chapter.

Comprehension — *Reviewing Important Facts*

Match the sentence in **Group A** with the word or phrase from **Group B** that the sentence explains. Write the letter of the correct answer on the blank.

Group A

_____ 1. We have more goods and services available to us than our parents had.

_____ 2. This gives us a higher standard of living.

_____ 3. Wise use of these leads to economic growth.

_____ 4. The first computer helped people do more work faster.

_____ 5. Gold is discovered in a country.

_____ 6. Smoke from factories makes the air dirty.

_____ 7. This is one problem caused by economic growth.

Group B

a. invention

b. cost of economic growth

c. higher standard of living

d. increase in resources

e. factors of production

f. economic growth

g. resources used up

Vocabulary — *Exclusions*

One word or phrase in each group does not belong. Find that word and cross it out. Then write a sentence that tells how the other words are alike.

1. more people at work
    lower taxes
    government has more money
    better government services

    _____

    _____

    _____

2. use of inventions
    wise use of resources
    increases in resources
    pollution

    _____

    _____

    _____

3. saving resources
   wasted money
   educated workers
   full use of machines,
      tools, and buildings
   _____
   _____
   _____
   _____

4. good tools
   a new oil field
   more labor
   a cleared forest
   _____
   _____
   _____

5. higher standard of living
   pollution
   increased crime
   used up resources
   _____
   _____

Critical Thinking – *Cause and Effect*

Choose a cause or an effect from **Group B** to complete each sentence in **Group A**. Write the letter of the correct answer on the blank.

Group A

1. Economic growth gives us many things

   our parents did not have, so _____ .

2. Economic growth requires more workers to produce the added goods and services,

   so _____ .

3. _____ , so it can do a better job of providing public goods.

4. _____ , so this resource will run out someday.

5. Many people left the farms and moved

   to the cities, so _____ .

Group B

a. More people working and paying taxes means the government has more money.

b. We have a higher standard of living.

c. The countries of the world use much oil.

d. Demand for houses, food, and clothing grew.

e. More people have jobs.

Comparing Costs of Items Using the Consumer Price Index

The table below is the Consumer Price Index for six different types of items from 1970 to 1990. Study the table. Then answer the questions.

Consumer Price Index, 1970 to 1990 1982 – 84 = 100					
Item	1970	1975	1980	1985	1990
Cereals and bakery products	37.1	62.9	83.9	107.9	140.0
Meats, poultry, fish, and eggs	44.6	67.0	92.0	100.1	130.0
Fuel oil	16.5	34.9	87.7	94.6	99.3
Piped gas and electricity	25.4	40.1	71.4	107.1	109.3
TV and sound equipment	(NA)	(NA)	100.7	91.9	(NA)
Energy	25.5	42.2	86.0	101.6	102.1

(NA means that information is not available.)

1. Which item shown had the lowest Consumer Price Index (CPI) in 1970?

2. Which item shown had the lowest CPI in 1990?

3. What was the CPI for meats, poultry, fish, and eggs in 1975?

4. Which group of foods shown had the largest increase in CPI between 1985 and 1990?

5. Did cereals and bakery products or energy costs increase the most between 1970 and 1990?

CHAPTER 16

Consider as you read

- What problems are there in the American economy?
- How can these problems be solved?

The United States has one of the strongest economies in the world. Its people have one of the highest standards of living in the world. Yet even this economy has some problems. Not everyone in America gets a fair "piece of the pie."

Equal Opportunity

Have you ever wanted tickets to a game or show that was sure to be sold out? Often tickets to such events are hard to get. You may have to stand in line for hours. Even then, the tickets may be gone before you reach the window. If this happens to you, you may feel that it is not fair. But look at it

People are in competition to get tickets to a concert. Everyone had an equal opportunity to get in line early.

159

another way. The people who got tickets came early. They were in line ahead of you. You could have come earlier. You had the same chance to be early that they did.

You and all the other people who wanted tickets were in competition with each other. In competition, some people win, and some people lose. This is what makes free enterprise work. However, free enterprise works best when competition is fair. Everyone must have the same chance to win. This is called **equal opportunity**.

Discrimination is the opposite of equal opportunity. There are laws against discrimination in the United States. It is against the law to refuse to give someone a job because of the person's race, sex, or religion. It is against the law for a bank to refuse to give credit to someone for these reasons. A school cannot refuse to educate people because they are African American, cannot speak English, or must use a wheelchair. These things still happen, however.

The damage done by discrimination is often hidden. For example, at one time women were not allowed to go to school to become doctors. Many women could have become very good doctors. Our country would have had better medical care. Perhaps people died because there were not enough

equal opportunity
giving everyone a fair chance

There are laws to allow everyone equal opportunity.

Today, people with disabilities are allowed to work at any job.

doctors. Some of the people who died might have done great things for our country. But we will never know.

Discrimination keeps people from doing their best. It means that there is less competition. Sometimes it means that the best person for a job does not get it. This can hurt many people other than the person who did not get the job. Suppose an airline would not hire African American pilots. Some of the African American pilots might have been better pilots than the people the airline did hire. If a plane crashed, many people would be killed. Perhaps a better pilot could have saved those people. If you were on that plane, wouldn't you want the best pilot flying it?

In the same way, any discrimination based on something other than a person's ability to do a job hurts the economy. If we do not have the best possible person in every job, time and money are wasted. Waste must be paid for by someone. Waste results in higher prices. Waste means that you must pay more for what you buy.

The United States is fighting discrimination. Laws have been passed against it. However, the battle is not won. We must see that the laws are fairly applied. Many groups in America must still fight for equal opportunity. These groups include African Americans, Hispanics, Asians, women, and people with disabilities.

The Farm Problem

American farmers are the best in the world. One farmer can grow enough food for sixty people. A hundred years ago, eighty out of every one hundred Americans lived on farms. Today only three out of every one hundred do. Yet this small number of people feeds not only America but much of the rest of the world.

You might think that farmers would be rich. However, this is not the case. Some farmers do make a lot of money. But most barely get by. The problem is that farmers do their jobs too well. They grow more food than can be sold. This causes prices to fall very low. The price of farm products is sometimes lower than the cost of growing the crops.

The heart of the farm problem is that there are too many farmers growing too many crops. The law of supply and demand tells us that when supply is greater than demand, prices will fall. When prices fall, producers are supposed to cut back on the supply. However, farmers keep on growing crops. Why? The answer is that the government helps them stay in business. It pays them to keep producing crops that nobody will buy.

Farming is big business in the United States. If all the farmers went out of business, the whole economy would be hurt. Therefore, the government tries to help farmers stay in business. The government has been trying to help farmers for more than fifty years. The idea is to help farmers make a profit. Then they will keep farming.

Only a few farmers are able to grow enough food for hundreds of people.

In Nebraska in 1985, farmers grew so much grain there was nowhere to store it. They had to pile the surplus grain on the main street.

The government has tried to help farmers mainly through **price supports**. The idea of price supports is to make sure that farmers are paid enough for their crops to make a profit.

Under price supports, the government bought surplus crops from farmers. The government had to pay to store all this food. It gave some food away to the needy. But much of the food was not used. Tax money was used to pay for this program. This cost Americans a great deal of money. Price supports also raised the prices people had to pay for food.

Price supports did not work well. Price supports helped farmers make a profit. This encouraged them to grow even more crops. This caused the price to fall even lower. But farmers continued to grow many crops. So the government paid them more money. This made up the difference between what the farmers spent to grow the crops and what they earned when they sold them.

Other ways to lower farm production have been tried. None have worked very well. A great deal of money has been spent to solve the farm problem. But after fifty years, the problem is still with us.

We all need food. If we did not have farmers, we would have to depend on other countries for food. In time of war, the supply could be cut off. It is important for our country to have farmers. So far, however, no one has found a way to help farmers without causing the farm problem to get even bigger.

price supports
payments made to businesses by the government

163

Vocabulary — *Writing With Vocabulary Words*

Use six or more words in the box to write a paragraph that tells how discrimination hurts free enterprise.

damage	discrimination	competition	refuse
free enterprise	equal opportunity	ability	waste

_____

_____

_____

_____

_____

_____

_____

_____

Comprehension — *Write the Answer*

Write one or more sentences to answer each question.

1. If someone gave you a job because you went to their church, would this be equal

   opportunity or discrimination? Explain. _____

   _____

   _____

2. How does competition help free enterprise? _____

   _____

3. What groups in America still do not enjoy equal opportunity? _____

_____

4. For how many people can one American farmer grow food? _____

_____

5. Why do many American farmers have trouble making a living? _____

_____

6. Why didn't government price supports work well? _____

_____

Critical Thinking – *Fact and Opinion*

Read each sentence below. If the sentence is a fact, write **F** on the blank. If the sentence is an opinion, write **O** on the blank. If the sentence gives both a fact and an opinion, write **FO** on the blank, and circle the part of the sentence that is an opinion.

_____ 1. Equal opportunity means that we all have the chance to compete fairly.

_____ 2. Some people should be discriminated against because they have not earned the right to be treated fairly.

_____ 3. The damage done by discrimination is often hard to see.

_____ 4. Discrimination can hurt the economy, but it isn't something we have to worry about.

_____ 5. It takes fewer farmers to feed America today than it did one hundred years ago.

_____ 6. Government programs to help farmers have not worked well, so the government should just leave farmers alone.

_____ 7. Price supports tried to make sure that farmers made a profit.

_____ 8. It is worth whatever it costs to keep American farmers in business.

_____ 9. Tax money was used to pay for price supports, but not enough was used.

_____ 10. The government has tried other ways to solve the farm problem.

The Great S&L Mess

Many Americans still remember the Great Depression of the 1930s. Thousands of banks failed. People who had money in those banks lost it all. Americans decided to make sure this never happened again. Laws were passed to insure money deposited in banks and savings and loans.

However, in the 1990s, banks and savings and loans again faced hard times. So many failed that the system of insurance itself was placed in danger. It cost as much as a billion dollars a day to keep America's savings and loans from going broke. Many banks failed as well. Americans were angry when they learned that taxpayers would have to pay as much as $2,000 to $4,000 each to save the banking industry.

How did this mess happen? It boils down to one main reason. Congress passed laws that made it possible. First, in 1980, Congress passed a law that let S&Ls pay whatever interest rates they wanted to. Until this time S&Ls could pay no more than 5.5 percent interest. The law also raised insurance coverage on deposits from $40,000 to $100,000. Next, in 1982, Congress passed a law that let S&Ls loan money for almost any purpose. These two laws took S&Ls out of the business of only loaning people money to buy houses, probably the safest kind of loan. It put them into the business of loaning people money to buy land and build huge buildings. Such loans are often very risky, but they pay high interest.

federal regulation
law made by the United States government

The 1982 law also let S&Ls loan as much money as an expert said a piece of land or a building was worth. "That **federal regulation** is what killed us dead," said a Texas government official. What happened next could almost have been predicted. Real estate developers bought S&Ls and then used them to finance risky deals. They paid experts to say land and buildings were worth

This Savings and Loan in Maryland closed in 1985.

far more than they actually were. If the deals went well, they could get rich. But if they failed, the federal deposit insurance would pay for the loss.

People whose main purpose was to make money for themselves were running S&Ls. One S&L owner in California bought "his and her" Rolls-Royces for himself and his girlfriend. One way they got money was by faking the building of apartments. They "paid" workers almost $6 million to "build" an apartment building that was nothing but a vacant lot. The $6 million disappeared into their pockets.

The lesson of the S&L mess was that there is a need for government regulation of banking. Given the opportunity to get rich at no risk to themselves, too many people were unable to resist doing things they knew they shouldn't. Not all were **criminals**. As one FBI agent put it, some of these people "were just too dumb to be in the banking business."

criminals
people who committed a crime

Write About It

On a separate sheet of paper, write a paragraph that tells whether you think the taxpayers should have to pay the cost of saving the banking industry and why.

In 1933, during the Great Depression, people waited in long lines to get cash from their bank.

UNIT 7

TRADE

The United States leads the world in trade. It buys and sells more goods with other countries than any other nation in the world. We get many things we need by trading with other nations. We get oil from Kuwait and cars from Japan.

But trade has its bad side, too. Buying goods from other countries means businesses in this country are hurt. If we buy many cars from Japan, then we are not buying as many cars that are built in Michigan. That might mean that factories in Michigan have to let some workers go. Or some factories might close down completely. This can hurt the economy in the United States.

Trade can have other hidden costs. Some countries are cutting down their forests to sell wood to other countries. These forests take many, many years to grow back. American farmers can produce food more cheaply than farmers in other countries. Selling that food at low prices puts farmers in other countries out of business. That hurts other nations. Then those nations may not have as much money to spend on goods and services from the United States.

As you can see, trade is not simple. Only when all the good and bad things about trade are added up can we tell what the real cost of trade is.

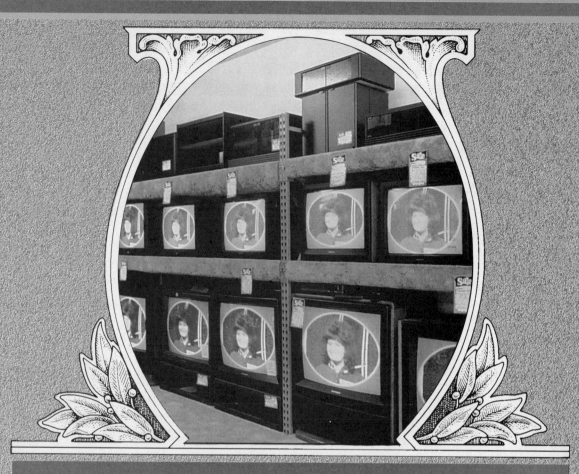

Have You Ever Wondered...

- Why are so many televisions and radios made in Japan?
- Why do nations trade with one another?
- How do we pay for the goods we buy from other countries?
- What do other countries have to do with you?
- How do nations decide what to produce?

This unit will answer such questions. You will learn why countries trade with each other. You will find out why the United States makes the kinds of things it does. You will read about efforts to make trade among nations easier. You will come to understand that your life is closely connected to people in many countries around the world.

INTERNATIONAL TRADE

CHAPTER 17

Consider as you read

- Why do some nations produce some goods and other nations produce others?
- How does the United States control trade with other nations?

Would you like to go on a shopping trip around the world? You don't have to win a contest. It's easy. Just go to almost any store. Look at the things that are for sale. Somewhere there will be a label or tag that tells you where the thing was made. Make a list of the different places. You will probably find things made all over the world.

You may already own things made in other countries. Clothes, cars, televisions, and radios are just a few of the things we buy that are often made in other countries. We can make all these things in the United States. Why, then, do we buy things made in other places? Why can't we always "buy American"?

Many goods for sale in the United States come from other nations.

A nation produces a good such as coffee if that nation has an absolute advantage in producing it.

Reasons for International Trade

International trade has been going on for thousands of years. Such trade began because people needed or wanted things that they could not get in their own country. Different countries have different resources. Some countries have gold. Others do not. Some countries can grow coffee. Others cannot.

Many countries have some amount of gold. But only a few countries have a lot of gold in one place that is easy to reach. In these countries the cost of mining gold is lower than it is in other countries. A country that can produce something by using few resources has an **absolute advantage**. It means that a country can produce an item at a lower cost than another country. Brazil has an absolute advantage over the United States in the growing of coffee. Brazil sells much coffee to the United States. To grow coffee in the United States, we would need to use a lot of water and build special buildings in which to grow the coffee. We would use the resources of water and building materials. The climate in Brazil is just right for growing coffee, so fewer resources would have to be used up.

Brazil chooses to do the thing it does best. This is called **specialization**. Most countries specialize in growing or making certain things. How does a country decide which things to specialize in? Each country looks at all the things that it could make. Perhaps it could make both cars and ships.

international trade
trade among nations

absolute advantage
the ability to produce a good by using fewer resources than any other country that could produce that good

specialization
the production of just one or very few products

171

But it can make a larger profit from making cars. It would not use as many resources making cars as it would making ships. The country is said to have a **comparative advantage** in making cars. A country that has a comparative advantage in making cars is better off making cars and using part of its profits to buy the ships it needs from a country that has a comparative advantage in making ships.

Each nation has some absolute advantages. It has some comparative advantages. Each nation tends to produce the things in which it has an advantage. It then trades with other countries for the things that those countries have an advantage in producing.

Countries depend on each other for the things they need. The United States depends on many countries for oil, cars, and other goods and resources. Other countries depend on the United States for wheat, computers, machines, and other goods. The need to buy and sell things among countries is what causes international trade.

Barriers to International Trade

You might think that countries would produce only those things in which they have an absolute or a comparative advantage and buy everything else from other countries.

Japan has a comparative advantage in producing cars. Many Japanese cars are sold in the United States.

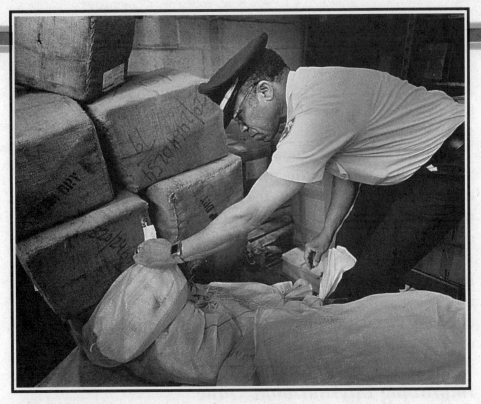

Goods that come into the United States are inspected.

However, it's not that simple. Countries limit trade. They do this to protect businesses from competition. They also limit trade to protect jobs and keep people working.

Tariffs are one way that countries limit trade. Tariffs are used to encourage people to buy goods made inside the country. They work this way. Suppose cars made in another country are cheaper than cars made in the United States. People buy the cheaper cars. American car makers sell fewer cars. Workers in car factories are thrown out of work. The United States can stop this by putting a tariff on cars made in other countries. This tax can be made so high that the cars from other countries would cost more than cars made in the United States. People would then be more likely to buy the American cars.

An **import quota** is another way to limit trade. For example, suppose the United States has an import quota on shoes. The quota will be set at a low amount — far less than the number of pairs of shoes Americans buy each year. This means that American shoe makers will sell most of the shoes sold in this country. Import quotas limit competition. They help protect businesses and jobs.

The strongest limit on trade is the **embargo**. Embargoes are not used to protect businesses or jobs. Embargoes are used to

tariffs
taxes on goods brought into a country

import quota
a limit put on the number of goods from one country that are brought into another country

embargo
a law that cuts off trade with another country

hurt other countries. The United States put an embargo on the sale of wheat to the Soviet Union in 1980. This was done to punish the Soviet Union for making war on another country.

Tariffs, quotas, and embargoes protect businesses and jobs. Some of the protected businesses are very important. For example, we need steel. We use steel in guns, tanks, and planes. We must have these things to protect ourselves. Other countries can make steel cheaper than the United States can. It would be cheaper to buy all our steel from other countries. But what might happen in case of war? Our supply of steel might be cut off. This could cause us to lose the war. We use tariffs and quotas to protect businesses that make the things we need.

Improving International Trade

Protecting one's own businesses and jobs sounds like a good idea. However, tariffs and quotas usually raise prices. This means that you, the consumer, have to pay more for goods. Your shoes may cost more because of an import quota on shoes. Your television may cost more because of a tariff on televisions.

Some people believe we should have **free trade**. No nation has completely free trade. However, some nations do work

free trade
trade that has no limits on it set by the government

These cars have arrived in the United States from another nation. They will soon be delivered to sellers around the country.

Many goods are carried across the border from Mexico to the United States, and from the United States to Mexico.

together to make trade easier. The United States will lower its tariffs with some nations. Other laws make it possible for the president to cut tariffs. Countries that want to sell goods in this country want tariffs cut. This will make their goods cheaper here. People will be more likely to buy them. Often, such countries will cut tariffs on American goods if the United States will lower tariffs on their goods. Naturally, the United States does this only when it will help this country.

The United States depends more on trade with some countries than it does with others. Some people feel we should have free trade with those countries. Two of these countries are Canada and Mexico. They need many of the things that are produced in the United States. The United States buys many of the things that they produce. The three countries depend on one another for trade. All three countries signed the North American Free Trade Agreement (NAFTA) in 1993. This agreement will help businesses in the United States sell goods to Canada and Mexico. It will also be easier for businesses in those countries to sell goods in the United States.

Free trade among all countries is not likely to happen. Each country feels that it must protect its own people first. However, countries will continue to try to improve trade whenever it helps them. One thing is certain — all the countries of the world need one another. In the next chapter, you will read about how the United States depends on trade with other countries.

Vocabulary — *Match Up*

Choose a word or phrase from the box to complete each sentence. Write that word or phrase on the blank.

import quota	**comparative advantage**	**free trade**	**embargo**
tariff	**absolute advantage**	**specialization**	

1. _____ means that Brazil can produce coffee cheaper than other countries can.

2. The production of just a few items is _____ .

3. When a country can produce several things cheaply, it uses

   _____ to decide what to specialize in.

4. A tax on goods brought into a country is a _____ .

5. If a country wants to be sure that only a certain amount of something is brought into

   a country, it can set an _____ .

6. To be sure that Americans did not trade at all with a certain country, the government

   could put an _____ on trade with that country.

7. Because all countries desire to protect jobs and businesses, no country

   has _____ .

Comprehension — *Write the Questions*

Below are the answers for some questions from this chapter. Read each answer. Then write your own questions above each answer. Use the question words to help you.

1. What _____ ?
   This began because people needed or wanted things they could not get in their own countries.

2. What _____ ?
   This lets a country produce something at a lower cost than another country.

3. What _____ ?

   This helps a country decide which things to specialize in.

4. How _____ ?

   It limits the amount of foreign goods sold in a country by making them cost more.

5. What _____ ?

   This is a limit on goods brought into a country.

6. What _____ ?

   It is a law used as a weapon to hurt other countries.

7. What _____ ?

   The United States, Mexico, and Canada signed this to make trade easier between the countries.

Critical Thinking — *Cause and Effect*

Choose a cause or an effect from **Group B** to complete each sentence in **Group A**. Write the letter of the correct answer on the blank.

Group A

1. _____ , so countries are a part of international trade.

2. Brazil has an absolute advantage over the United States in growing coffee, so _____ .

3. Russia has large supplies of gold that are easy to mine, so _____ .

4. _____ , so the United States is a major supplier of grain to the world.

5. Countries feel they must protect their businesses and jobs, so _____ .

6. _____ , so it put an embargo on the sale of wheat to that country.

Group B

a. It has an absolute advantage in the production of gold.

b. Large parts of this country are ideal for growing corn and wheat.

c. They limit trade.

d. The United States buys this item rather than growing it itself.

e. The United States wanted to punish the Soviet Union.

f. All countries do not have everything they need.

177

Reading a Zero-Line Graph

The graph below shows the balance of trade in the United States from 1970 to 1990. Study the graph. Then answer the questions.

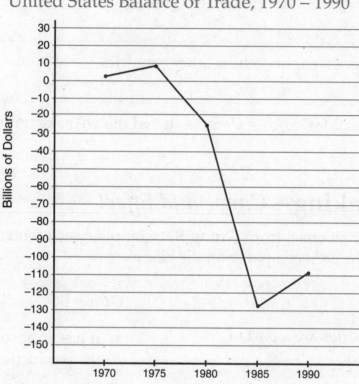

United States Balance of Trade, 1970 – 1990

1. What does the number 1980 stand for on the scale that runs across the bottom of the graph? _____

2. What does the number 20 stand for on the scale that runs along the left side of the graph? _____

3. In what years shown did the United States have a balance of trade that was greater than zero? _____

4. In what year shown was the balance of trade in the United States the greatest amount less than zero? What was the figure for that year? _____

_____

5. What was the balance of trade in the United States in 1990? _____

_____

CHAPTER 18

Consider as you read

- What kind of trade does the United States have with other countries?
- How does trade affect the economy?

You may think that you do not depend on other countries. However, a close look at your daily life will show otherwise. Let's spend a few hours with a consumer and see how she depends on other countries. As you read, think about your own life.

Beth, our consumer, wakes up to the sound of music from her clock radio. It was made in Korea. She turns on her coffee maker. It was made in Germany. The coffee came from Brazil. She eats fruit grown in Mexico.

Most televisions sold in the United States come from Japan.

179

Getting ready for work, Beth puts on jeans made in Taiwan and a blouse from Hong Kong. Her belt is from Guatemala. Her shoes were made in Italy.

On her way to work (in an American car put together in Canada), Beth stops for gas. The gasoline was made from oil from Nigeria and Saudi Arabia. There is to be a party at work today, so Beth buys a tin of cookies. They were made in Denmark.

Before she even gets to work, Beth has used products from a dozen countries besides the United States. Like Beth, we all depend on other countries for many of the things we use every day. This chapter will help you understand why.

Economic Advantages of the United States

The United States has great natural resources. It has many skilled workers. It makes use of many machines and inventions to do work. The land, labor, and capital of the United States give it advantages in producing certain goods.

Food is one of the things that the United States produces best. American farmers can grow some crops more cheaply

The United States produces huge amounts of wheat and other grains.

Here, wheat is being loaded onto a ship so that it can be exported.

than they can be grown anywhere else in the world. The United States grows about half the world's corn. It grows large amounts of wheat, sorghum, and soybeans. The United States has an absolute advantage in the production of these crops.

The United States is also a world leader in manufacturing. This is made possible by its many natural resources, its skilled labor, and its use of machines and inventions. America leads the world in the manufacture of clothing. It also produces many machines, cars, chemicals, metals, and computers.

The United States is able to manufacture almost anything. However, it has a comparative advantage in producing certain things such as medicines, fertilizers, plastics, and airplanes. Businesses are able to make more money producing these things than they would if they made other things. The United States sells these things to other countries and uses the money to buy the things that it needs.

Imports and Exports

Of all the wheat sold in international trade, the United States sells about four pounds in ten. It sells seven of every ten pounds of corn, sorghum, and soybeans sold in the world. Food is an important **export** of the United States.

Machinery is the largest single export of the United States. This group of goods includes planes, cars and trucks, and

export
a good sold to another country

181

computers. Chemicals are another large export. Medicines, fertilizers, and plastics are all made from chemicals. Raw materials, such as wood, metals, and oils from seeds and nuts, are other important exports.

The United States also buys many goods from other countries. It may surprise you to learn that the United States **imports** many of the same things it exports. For example, the United States imports many cars and trucks. The reason is that some people like those cars better than the ones made in America.

Foods such as fish, vegetables, and fruits are large imports of the United States. So are oil, machines, computers, clothing, steel, shoes, toys, and sporting goods.

The United States is very dependent on other countries. It must sell goods. It must buy other goods. The United States must buy some things that it needs from other countries. For example, the United States has few of some minerals and none of others. Some of these minerals are very important for manufacturing some goods in the United States. So it must buy those minerals.

imports
brings goods from one country into another country

Lumber from the United States is being loaded onto a ship for export.

Gasoline, which may have come from oil from the Middle East, is being delivered to a gas station.

The United States also buys some things that it cannot produce enough of. Oil is perhaps the most important. The United States must import from one third to almost one half of all the oil it uses. This oil runs our cars and heats our homes. Without oil, the United States economy would almost come to a stop. This makes us very dependent on the countries that have oil.

The United States also imports things that other countries have an absolute advantage in producing. Japan, for example, has long had an absolute advantage in producing radios and televisions. As a result, most televisions and radios sold in the United States are made in Japan or other countries.

Balancing Payments and Trade

When you eat at a restaurant, you may have a nice meal followed by dessert. But after dessert comes the bill. You must pay for the things you enjoyed.

Countries collect money for the things that they sell. Of course, they must pay for the things they buy, too. Our government keeps track of all the things the United States buys and sells. For many years, the United States has bought and sold more goods than any other country.

Countries like to take in more money than they spend. It is easy to see why. Think of yourself. You need to earn more money than you spend. If you do not, you must borrow money to make up the difference. The same is true of countries.

Countries try to export enough goods to make all the money that they need to pay for all their imports. Each year, countries add up how much they took in from selling goods to other countries and how much they paid out to buy goods from other countries. The difference between the two amounts is the country's **balance of trade**. A country that has money left over after it pays for all its imports has a favorable balance of trade. A favorable balance of trade means the country took in more money for exports than it spent on imports. An unfavorable balance of trade means that the country spent more than it took in.

For more than twenty years now, the United States has had an unfavorable balance of trade. Because Americans buy so many imported goods, American businesses have been hurt. Hundreds of thousands of Americans have lost their jobs. The

balance of trade
the difference between the value of a country's imports and exports

Oil must be cleaned before it can be used.

184

As consumers, we all play an important role in the economy.

United States has had to borrow money to pay for the things it buys. This money has come from other countries. Today, many large companies in the United States are owned by people in other countries. People in other countries own a great deal of land in the United States.

People disagree over what to do. Some people feel that we must get back to a favorable balance of trade. Others feel that it is more important for consumers to get the things they need and want at the lowest possible price.

You will play an important part in deciding what happens. Each time you buy, you vote with your dollars. What you buy has economic impact around the world. You are part of the "invisible hand" guiding the world market. But you can also be lifted or crushed by that hand. That is why it is important for you to understand your place in the world economy.

Vocabulary — *Exclusions*

One word or phrase in each group does not belong. Find the word and cross it out. Then write a sentence that tells how the other words are alike.

1. land
   labor
   capital
   import

2. radios and televisions
   oil
   coffee
   grain

3. medicines
   fertilizers
   plastics
   wood

4. corn
   wheat
   soybeans
   coffee

Comprehension — *Write the Answer*

Write one or more sentences to answer each question.

1. What are three things the United States has an absolute advantage in producing?

2. What are three things the United States has a comparative advantage in producing?

3. Give three reasons the United States has advantages in manufacturing certain goods. _____

_____

4. Name five things the United States imports in large amounts. _____

_____

_____

5. If the United States can manufacture televisions and radios, why is almost every television and radio sold in the United States made in another country?

_____

6. What does it mean when we say the United States has an unfavorable balance of trade? _____

_____

Critical Thinking — *Drawing Conclusions*

Read the paragraph below and the sentences that follow it. Put a check in front of the conclusions that can be drawn from the paragraph.

> The United States has great natural resources. It has skilled workers. It uses many machines. It can manufacture almost anything. The United States also grows many crops better than any other country. It has a great many imports and exports.

_____ 1. The United States is probably a great manufacturing nation.

_____ 2. Most of the things the United States makes are made from its own natural resources.

_____ 3. Food is an important product of the United States.

_____ 4. Exports of food pay for most of the things the United States imports.

_____ 5. Since it can manufacture or grow so many things, the United States should have a favorable balance of trade.

_____ 6. The United States trades a great deal with other countries.

The Global Pencil

You have thousands of people all over the world working for you. People around the world are working in mines and factories and on farms to produce things you need. Ships and planes are crossing the oceans to bring these things to you.

All people, all over the world, work for each other. We all depend on others for things we cannot make for ourselves. We are all interdependent.

Something as simple as a pencil shows how much we depend on people in other countries. It takes thousands of people from as many as twenty different countries and states to make one little pencil.

Much of the wood for pencils comes from trees in Oregon. The chain saw that cut the trees may have been made in Japan. The gasoline to run it started out as crude oil from Texas, Mexico, Alaska, or Saudi Arabia.

The logs are loaded onto a truck made in Michigan and taken to a sawmill in California. The logs are sawed into small pieces before being sent to a factory in Pennsylvania. Pencil lead is mostly graphite. Graphite comes from mines in Sri Lanka, a country just south of India. A ship built in Japan, owned by a person who lives in France, and run by a company that does business from Liberia, brings the graphite to the United States. The graphite is mixed with clay from Mississippi and wax from Mexico.

The rubber in the eraser probably comes from Malaysia. The gritty stuff in the eraser is pumice. Pumice comes from volcanoes in Italy. The piece of metal that holds the eraser onto the pencil is brass. Brass is made of zinc and copper. Zinc comes mainly from Canada, Australia, Russia, and Ireland. The copper may have come from Bolivia, Chile, or Zambia.

These logs were cut down in the state of Washington.

The pencil must be painted. Castor oil in the paint comes from plants in Africa. After the pencil is painted, the name of the maker is stamped on it. The black paint has carbon black from Texas in it.

Hundreds of other people are involved in shipping and selling the pencil after it leaves the factory. No matter where you live, people in any one of the fifty states could play a part in providing you with a pencil.

All those countries and all those thousands of people work together just so you can write!

❖

Write About It

On a separate sheet of paper, write a paragraph that tells how things you do affect people in other countries.

The machine that lifts the logs was made in Oregon.

Vocabulary List

Index